Accelerate Your Success With The Internet

The
Electronic
Dream

Essential
Ingredients
For Growing
A People
Business
In An
e-Commerce
World

D0121916

JOHN FUHRMAN

The Electronic Dream

John Fuhrman
Email rejectme@aol.com
Copyright ©2000 by John Fuhrman
ISBN 0-938716-61-1

Published by
Possibility Press
e-mail: PossPress@aol.com

Manufactured in the United States of America

Dedication

For all of you who are excited by the increasing potential available to you as the world embraces e-commerce. Use it to build a bright future for yourself and your family. The possibilities for your success are enormous.

Acknowledgements

First of all, I thank God for inspiring me. And thanks to my loving family—my wife Helen, son John, and daughter Katie. You have all been tremendously supportive and understanding while I worked on this book.

Thanks to all of you who have carried the "torch" of helping people realize their potential and live their dreams. I have learned life-changing principles from many of you and have been inspired to carry the torch as well, in the best way I know how.

Thanks much to my publisher, who believed in me when a hundred others didn't, and the editors and staff who all helped make this book what it is. I couldn't have done it without you.

Thanks to the scientists, engineers, and entrepreneurs who developed the computer, the Internet and e-commerce.

Thanks to the people who pioneered this great industry, including the corporate suppliers and the leaders who developed the system of success that has made this business the great opportunity that it is today.

And finally, a great big thank you to my hero and former neighbor, the late Og Mandino, who inspired me to enter the writing and speaking profession.

Contents

Prologue

"By helping enough people grow and use the Internet to improve their financial picture, you can generate a lifetime of residual income that can even be passed on to your heirs."

As I was writing this book on my computer, I took a break and listened to my voice mail. There was a message from a business associate of mine explaining the true insecurity of today's job market. Even in a booming economy, companies are looking for ways to cut expenses and improve their performance for their stockholders.

My associate shared that a corporate vice president had been let go from his job. This scenario is all too common these days, so it's not earth-shattering news. However, I believe the way it happened is a wake-up call. This man walked into his office to start his day, and went over to the fax machine. And much to his dismay, there was his dismissal notice! Nothing personal, mind you, just a machine delivering a termination notice! And it didn't even include a "Thanks for all you've done for us."

You may be thinking, "How cold," or "How impersonal." And that is why I'm sharing this example — to prove two points. First, when companies are more interested in "the bottom line" than in the people who helped create that same line, people are typically cast aside as soon as someone *or something* can do it for less money. The tasks the ousted person was responsible for may not even have to be done as well, just in a reasonably acceptable manner, as long as the cost is lower.

The second point is to demonstrate the "efficiency" of technology, when left to carry out a task by itself. While it is true the computer is able to deliver the message with incredible accuracy, can help ship products on time, and calculates payments due—"down to the third decimal point"—it's still the human element that's most important. That's what keeps people returning to do more business and ultimately leads to referrals.

The information age is exploding. People are becoming wealthy by sharing the idea of using the Internet to help distribute goods, services, and information. You too have the opportunity to participate and profit from this new technology. But you'll be successful only if you use the most powerful ingredient in this new aspect of the business—*you!* You are the essential element in this high-tech picture. To reach your financial goals with this business, you need to be an active ingredient. You need to be *the* instrument that delivers the message of opportunity.

When you take on that responsibility, you can reap rewards that may now seem almost too good to be true. By helping enough people grow and use the Internet to improve their financial picture, you can generate a lifetime of residual income that can even be passed on to your heirs.

Using this opportunity, coupled with the power of the Internet, makes this an exciting business for virtually anyone who is looking for a chance at a better life, and is willing to work for it.

The main objective of this book is to expose you to the awesome power of the Internet, while helping you to understand that all that power won't do you much good if you think it's going to accomplish your goals without you. However, with effort and commitment on your part — along with a big dream — this powerful ally can be used as a tool for you to get to the top.

Food For Thought

An elderly carpenter was finally ready to retire. He told his employer-contractor of his plans to leave the house-building business and live a more leisurely life with his extended family. He shared that they would miss the paycheck, but nonetheless, he still wanted to retire. He reassured his boss that they could "get by."

The contractor was sorry to see his good worker go and asked if he could build just one more house as a personal favor. The carpenter said "yes," but in time it was easy to see that his heart was not in his work. He resorted to quick, shoddy workmanship and used inferior materials. It was an unfortunate way to end his career.

When the carpenter finished his work, the builder came to inspect the house. But instead of checking his employee's work, the contractor handed the front door key to the carpenter. "This is your house," he said, "my gift to you for all your years of loyal service."

What a shock! If only the carpenter had known he was building his own house, he would have done it all so differently. Now he was about to live in a home he had built none too well.

And so it could be with many other people. Perhaps they are building their lives in a distracted way, reacting rather than acting, and willing to put up with less than the best. At important points in their lives, they may not give their jobs or businesses their best effort. Then with a shock, as they later look at the situation they have created, they find they are now living in the "house" they have built—which they are not pleased with!

If they had realized that at the beginning, they would have done it differently. Think of yourself as a carpenter building your life. Think about the "house" you are building. Each day as you hammer a nail, place a board, or erect a wall, build wisely. Your future depends on it.

It is the only life you will ever build. Even if you live it for only one more day, you deserve to live that day graciously and with dignity. As the plaque on the wall says, "Life is a do it yourself project."

How could it be said more clearly? Your life today is largely the result of the attitudes you held and the choices you made in the past. And your life tomorrow will be primarily the result of your current attitudes and the choices you make today. It's all up to you.

Introduction

"The power of the Internet offers a golden opportunity to attract millions of people who weren't previously interested, or perhaps were never exposed to the business in the first place."

I remember the spring of 1973. After being accepted to engineering school, my father bought me my first calculator. You should have seen the buttons — sine, co-sine, tangent, square roots, and reciprocals. Oh yes, it even did multiplication, division and other simple math.

Now some of you may not understand the above geometric, algebraic, or trigonometric terms, but the calculator can be used to solve problems of that nature. However, if *you* didn't already understand the fundamentals of working with these types of problems, it wouldn't do you much good to have the calculator.

Just having buttons to push won't do you much good. It will never enable you to accomplish what someone can achieve who understands *why* certain buttons need to be pushed to do what they do. But once you gain that understanding, using such an electronic tool can put you considerably ahead of the game. You would then be using it to accelerate your progress, while not expecting it to be a replacement for knowledge and understanding. The calculator is valuable because it's convenient and saves you time and energy.

This book is designed to give you a clear understanding of some business basics so that you can most effectively use e-commerce to accelerate yourself toward your dreams and goals. Mastering the fundamentals will enable you to use the new technology with a clear understanding of how it can enhance an already proven process.

You need to understand that technology is a powerful tool. But it will *never* replace the key elements of success in this business, or any business, for that matter. It will *never* do the work you need to do to achieve your goals and dreams. It is not just the push of a button and out comes instant success.

The Internet offers a golden opportunity to *attract* millions of people who weren't previously interested or perhaps were never exposed to the business in the first place. It can enable you to convey your message of "dream reaching" with the click of a button. But the key element always remains — *you*.

You need to be accessible. You need to be available, sincerely interested in the success of others, and willing to do what it takes to help them succeed. This new technology can help you take your dreams from possibility to reality. But, without you and a committed effort on your part, it could become little more than a business video game.

Have you ever noticed that the greatest pieces of advice or solutions to challenges are often the simplest? This book is to provide you with simple solutions, sound advice, and the information you need to motivate yourself to put into action what you're about to read.

Regardless of the technology available or the knowledge you've obtained, you still need to take the necessary actions to achieve your goals and dreams. Otherwise, you'll just be left with wishful thinking — wondering what it would have been like if you had done what you could have to make it happen for yourself.

If you are just looking at this business and start getting excited by the possibilities, here's what you may want to do: First, get back with the person who shared this book with you and thank them for doing so. They apparently saw something in you that you may not even have noticed yourself. It seems they had confidence in your abilities. It's likely they wanted to share this book so you could have a real opportunity to reach your full potential, using both the power of the Internet and working with other people.

Next, repeat the process. Show the person who shared this with you that *you* now understand one of the key secrets to success — *sharing* your newfound knowledge with others. Share your excitement with someone who may be looking to better themselves — someone who has a dream for a better life. Perhaps they have talents they haven't discovered and need someone like you to help them find and develop them. Perhaps they have dreams too, but no way to make them come true. You can give them the good news — you've found a way. Your real growth, both personally and professionally, will come from sharing with others as much as you possibly can.

> *"When you open your hand for giving,*
> *you also open it to receive more."*

Chapter One

Life Is A Contact Sport

"Meeting new people and building relationships is the key to growing your business. Once that is done, the power of using the Internet can be shared and multiplied."

Safe Or Successful?

Technology is changing — faster and faster every day. By the time I installed my most recent computer, much of its technology was already becoming obsolete! Keeping up with these changes is like pushing water up a hill. Some of it gets there but most of it goes right through our fingers.

When things seem to be going right past us at a rapid rate, some people may feel *safe* by focusing only on what they know. They may hold on tightly to what they already have. They could even begin to feel "comfortable." They might not realize they're stuck in a rut. Perhaps they're even ignoring what is now happening with the Internet and calling it a "passing fancy" — just a fad—something that won't last.

Opportunities just seem to pass them by as they withdraw into their familiar zone, like a turtle into his shell.

They begin creating a sense of security when, in reality, there may not be any — especially if they work for somebody else. They look at where they've been as where they'll always be and feel secure that no one can take that away from them.

They ignore the fact that others are losing their jobs, perhaps all around them. They fail to understand that the very people who make them feel secure by signing their paycheck are the same ones who can "pull the rug out from under them" and rob them of their so-called security. They deny the reality that when employers embrace new technology, they often replace people who don't understand it with people who do, and even pay them less!

There is an enormous amount of new knowledge developing every day — at the fastest pace ever known to mankind. However, as with all knowledge gained since time began, it's not necessary to learn it all to succeed. Thank goodness! Successful people know this and often align themselves with other experts who have the knowledge they need. That way, the information is available to them whenever they need it.

What's so unique about what you're reading about is this: You don't need to hire an expert to help you improve your financial picture through this opportunity. They, or someone connected to them, may come to you because you may have expressed a desire to move on. Or maybe you have some winning qualities that struck a chord with them. For example, you might have a great attitude, or maybe you carry an air of credibility and honest ambition. Or, you may have what is one of the greatest assets in this business — teachability.

It's What You Don't See That Makes A House Stand Strong

They're constantly coming out with better materials to make a house last longer between paintings and reroofings. Insulation, high-tech heating units, and newly designed windows all keep you warmer during the winter. There are even appliances like hot tubs that can even take remote control orders from you while you're on your way home in your car! But there is one thing they cannot change without risking the stability of the structure. The foundation.

Buried from your sight is the true strength of most homes today. The foundation is what keeps a house from moving off its original site and crumbling to the ground. The foundation keeps the home from settling to one side or the other. And its strength allows you to add to it in the future, while still maintaining its integrity.

This business has many similarities to a well-built house. A solid structure was developed that has been built upon since the late 1950's. There have been additions to the business and improvements in many aspects of it. But the heart and strength of the business — its foundation — remains as solid as it was on the first day of operation.

Things can always be made better without sacrificing the original intent or integrity of the operation. One of the many laws of business, as well as in life, is that you either get better or else you'll get worse. There is no staying the same. There's no such thing as status quo. When technology advances, you either embrace it or you become a part of history.

This is your chance to take part in the future — as it unfolds. You have an opportunity to use the latest e-commerce business tools available without having to invest in a whole new education. You have the advantage of being able to get the help you need, when you need it, without going back to school, like many people in other industries do.

The Secret Of A Strong Business

Several years ago, I had a goal to get my first book published. Simple enough. I began seeking publishers who would agree to do it. One by one, they all said, "No." After 50 rejections I could have stopped and most people who know me would have consoled me with a bunch of, "Hey, you tried." After 75 they might have reacted by saying, "What else could you do?" Even after 100 they may have remarked that I went the "extra mile."

They missed the point. I wasn't seeking answers. I was looking for a publisher. Since there would be a contract involved, I could only work with one at a time. It didn't matter what 100 of them said. I was only looking for one who would publish my book. To this day I know that the only reason I was able to become a successful author was because I made the commitment to keep going until I got the answer I wanted. There are thousands of publishing companies out there. I was looking only for one!

Suppose I told you that you could enjoy a lifetime of freedom and success once you built a large business? Also, suppose that a large business was made up of 10,000 people. How would you feel? If you feel intimidated by the thought of having to find 10,000 people, just hang in there and relax. That's a perfectly normal feeling.

The secret to achieving success is sometimes so simple it's often overlooked. When you build your business you can't start at 9,999 and add one. You can't even start at 50. *Your* successful business begins when *you* get inspired and say, "Yes." *You can't climb the mountain of your dreams by starting near the peak. You begin with that first step at the bottom. That's where all success begins.*

You then focus on how each additional step, or person who joins you, brings you closer to your objective. And as you grow yourself and your business you will realize that these first people become a part of your foundation. But make no mistake about it, *you* are the essence of your own success. *You* are the cornerstone of your foundation.

It's Easier To Save A Dime Than A Dollar

"As soon as I have money I'm going to start saving." Have you ever heard or even said that yourself? I did. Then one day, after years of not having a savings account, the "lightbulb" went on. I realized that I needed to start saving before I could have any savings! Not the other way around — plain and simple. I also learned that it's easier to start small and work your way up. In fact, there's really no other way to do it. Unless, of course, you win the lottery or inherit a lot of money.

It's that way with running a business, too. If you can see yourself building a large business with thousands of people, you can also see yourself successfully leading them. Where did those skills come from? Certainly you would have learned from the leaders who came before you what's important to do. But remember, consistently putting what you've learned into practice is what will keep your business growing.

In the conventional business or job world you need to have the attitude that you are always training your replacement. You either train them to the best of your ability and, when it's time for you to be replaced, that person is ready and you're promoted. Or, you do nothing but protect the job you have and one day you may find your replacement has arrived and you're out. It's a choice that you make.

When you're building a business of your own, these same principles apply. You need to be training people to lead in your place — to duplicate you — as your business grows. The best way to do that is to begin training the very first person you sponsor into your business — *yourself.* It all begins with you. And this training becomes continuous as you add more people along the way.

Listen Carefully—You May Be Hearing Your Own Success Calling You!

Sometimes great discoveries happen "by accident." And on occasion you make changes in your life because you've learned a valuable lesson from the proverbial "school of hard knocks." Once you've learned it though, you need to share it with as many people as you can.

Dean was a good friend of mine. We had known each other for years and were even working together for a time. Without telling him, I began building a business of my own. I was having some success but it never occurred to me to invite him to take a look at it. But fortunately for him, he invited himself without either of us knowing it.

One day Dean and I were having lunch, talking about his job. He told me that the hours were really taking a toll on his life and his family. The money was good but there was virtually no time to do much of anything outside of his job. It had basically consumed his waking hours. He "owed his soul to the company store," as the old song goes. In fact, he told me that if he could figure out a way to make an extra few hundred dollars a month, he'd leave his then current job and get one with less hours. So, what do you suppose I did?

I left! After we finished eating I wished him luck and took off for home. An hour later, when I got home, I suddenly realized what I had done — or rather, didn't do. I had missed an opportunity to potentially help a friend get his life back, but I must have been so preoccupied with my own thoughts that I never *heard* him say he needed any help. And I didn't know how to tell him without embarrassing myself.

A week went by and what had happened that day at lunch kept gnawing at me. He was a friend and I had something that might help him improve his life. Finally it hit me. I called him up and asked him if he was serious about what he said. I also asked him if he would really quit his current job and get a new one with fewer hours, if he could find a way to earn some extra money? Finally I asked him, "What would you be willing to do to get it?"

When he told me he was ready to listen to just about anything that might offer some hope, I knew I had made the right decision. Rather than trying to *sell* him on the business, I told him that I *may* have something for him, but I wasn't sure it would be a good fit. At any rate, I told him I'd be happy to sit down and explore the possibilities with him.

Well, he did become part of my business and began learning what he needed to do to earn the extra income he wanted. But I was the one who really got the lesson! From that day on, I endeavored to spend more time *listening* to people. They'll tell you what they want to do with their lives. Just listen to them. After you do, the door could swing wide open for you to share what you're doing and how the Internet is involved. Then, things could get very exciting!

"In-home shopping is currently a $230 billion a year industry."

Entrepreneur Magazine

Chapter Two

This Opportunity Is "Ground Floor"

"When someone starts their business they are laying the foundation. They're also offering others the opportunity to be in on the ground floor of their own business, using the latest electronic technology."

"Adding To" Is Not The Same As Replacing

Whenever successful companies develop new ways to grow, they don't destroy whatever has helped them succeed to that point. They understand that what they've already accomplished needs to serve as a solid foundation on which to build their future. They realize that it's often just a small adjustment or a slight change of focus that can take them to new, unheard of levels of success. And that's what the power of the Internet represents to this business. It's adding a technology that can lead you to spectacular growth.

It's like wanting to climb to a certain height, using boxes you've piled one on top of the other. If each box represented an addition to your solid foundation, you would be closer to your goal as you piled another box on top of what was already solidly in place. However, if every time you had a new box and replaced the top box with it, you wouldn't accomplish much of anything. You'd just forever be standing on a new box. You'd be constantly starting over — never building on the strong, proven foundation already in place.

What makes a company successful is building a strong foundation. First of all, it's knowing that people are its greatest resource, and the importance of caring about them, meeting their needs, and treating them properly. This includes employees, customers, and the independent businesspeople they're associated with, perhaps to distribute the goods and services as well as share the opportunity.

Second to the people focus is the constant willingness to change and adapt to advancements in technology, as well as the intelligence to build upon past successes, while learning from previous setbacks. Change for the sake of change seldom accomplishes anything — while growth without change is impossible, as is growth without new people.

He Who Hesitates Is Lost!

In 1987 the New York Stock Exchange was hovering around the 2,000 mark. People everywhere were feverishly buying in because it was "going through the roof." Then one October day it came tumbling down — 500 points. Approximately 25 percent of the market's value vanished. People wondered if it would ever recover.

By 1993 the market was cruising again. When it reached the 5,000 mark many people got scared. They thought that growth was all the economy could possibly handle. Many began seeking safer investments while they waited for the "inevitable crash." Well, as you may recall, the crash never came.

As we enter the new millenium, the Dow Jones Industrial Average has already surpassed the 11,000 mark. In only 12 years it had increased over 500 percent, while doubling in the last few years of the 20th century. What will happen next? For many people the answer is *nothing!* While some people get involved and make things happen, many wait and see. And isn't it curious how the ones who choose just to wait and see often wonder why nothing spectacular ever seems to happen to them? Have you ever heard the expression, "He who hesitates is lost"?

Tops and bottoms, similar to those of the stock market, have also occurred in real estate, business growth, and even technology. Some people became tremendously successful in each of those arenas while most people could only say, "If only I had…"

The point is, there is always a ground floor when new technology is involved. By using the power of the Internet to help you build your business, you are on the cutting edge of what's happening in the world today. The problem most people have is that they hesitate to take advantage of any opportunity — ground floor, or anything else, for that matter. They ponder on what the correct timing will be. Often they analyze themselves into a stupor. If only they had invested that same time and energy into taking advantage of a fine opportunity, like this one is, they could be a lot better off.

There is only one answer that'll help you get where you want to go. *Get started now!* Catch the crest of the wave.

Focus On Where You Want To Go

Did you ever see someone you've admired and then had the chance to meet them? Did you feel intimidated? If so, that's perfectly normal. Especially if that person has the type of success you'd like to have — perhaps almost more than anything. You see such people, often after years of growing and becoming how they are now, and you may be comparing yourself where you are now to them, at their level.

You need to understand how unfair that is to yourself. It's like comparing a major league baseball star to a Little Leaguer. If you were just beginning your journey of success, why would you compare yourself with someone who's arrived at where you want to be? It's great to see what you can become and to keep that dream in your sights. But to decide whether or not you have the ability to grow into a person who achieves that kind of success, based on where you are now, as compared to them could be discouraging.

The beauty of this business is that while you get to see wonderfully successful people who are at the level you are aspiring to achieve, you can also listen to what they went through on their way there. They'll share where they started from and how they grew over time and through many setbacks, to arrive at where they are today. You may also discover that some of them were even in worse shape, financially and otherwise, than you when they got in the business.

Comparing yourself to others is dangerous in any personal journey. It can be such a self-esteem deflator. There will always be those who are doing better than you and, of course, those who are doing worse than you. Seeing how you stack up against others is not a good indicator as to whether or not *you* can succeed. In fact, you may surpass those you're tempted to compare yourself with — if only you'd stay focused on where *you want to go* and not where you are.

The only comparison that may prove helpful is you with yourself. It's perfectly fine and even necessary to look back and see where you've come from and compare it to where you are now and where you want to be tomorrow. How else can you gauge your progress? See and appreciate how much you've grown and developed as a person. Look at things you can now accomplish with ease that you may have thought impossible when you first got started. Focus on where you'd like to be, keep "piling up those boxes," and use them to get to the top.

If You're Not Now Planning Your Future... You Already Did

"Hey, I'm doing okay. I pay my bills. Get a raise every year. I even like my job." Sound familiar? If some or all of that sounds a little too close to home, you may be in for some trouble. As long as you believe things will just keep rolling along, you may be surprised and find the road to success and security has more than a few potholes. You may be in for a rocky ride.

Here in the U.S. we are currently experiencing a strong economy. Nonetheless, every day 3,000 people are being downsized, right-sized, laid-off, disemployed, or whatever the word of the day is for being put out of work — or "fired," to be less politically correct and more blunt. Others are being asked to work extra hours every week, often without extra pay, to make up for the gap in productivity from the loss of employees — often good loyal ones who worked hard.

People are also living longer than ever before. This is great news on one hand. However, on the flip side, this fact is creating a whole new set of challenges. How can you be sure you'll have enough money to live on when you'll probably live longer than you thought? If you've made no provisions for the extra years you could still be alive, then the question could be, "Who will take care of you?"

For the first time in history, adult children are faced with a situation that almost never existed in the past. Many of these people are barely finding a way to get their kids through college without bankrupting themselves. In many cases, they not only have little or no resources set aside for retirement, they are now faced with the added possibility of having to care for one or more of their parents. Their "empty nest" may not stay empty long and their so-called carefree years are often far from it.

Even though the economy is in really great shape, well over one million people will declare bankruptcy during the next twelve months. While that number may be disturbing to some of you, what disturbs me even more is the fact that many of them could have avoided that situation if only they had an extra $300 a month in income!

To earn an extra $300 a month you simply start with the decision to do so. Many people don't make plans because they often believe their financial situation is too far-gone to bother. Actually, quite the opposite is true.

We need to stop thinking in terms of how difficult things appear to be and begin looking for little ways, step by step, to make them better. Being a part of this business, especially since the Internet has been added, now gives everyone who decides to, a chance to change their financial picture.

If you make an effort to improve in some aspect of your life, say 1 percent a day, it's likely you'll be amazed at the results. In just 70 days your situation will be twice as good as it was, or over two times better than when you started! (This comes from multiplying 1.01 by itself 70 times.)

One step toward what you want may not seem like much. But, it brings you closer to where you want to be and further away from what you'd like to leave behind. Even one small step is worth the effort. Once you get going, keep going and the momentum of improvement can build.

The Dilution Solution

When you add water to any other liquid, that liquid becomes diluted. Diluting something diminishes its strength.

It weakens whatever the original solution was capable of doing. Even acid, diluted enough, can be made ineffective.

Suppose there is a drink you really enjoy. On a hot day you really look forward to grabbing a glass and filling it up with your favorite ice-cold beverage. Imagine that you are only allowed to put 5 percent of your favorite drink into the glass and you have to mix it with 95 percent water. How do you think it would taste? Would you even want to drink it?

Ninety-five percent of the people in the U.S. are either dead or dead broke by the time they are 65 years old. If you want a better life for yourself and your family, or anything else, why on earth would you continue doing what those people have always done—and dilute your success?

To get different results, you need to do something different from what the majority of people do, right? This is especially important when you look at the choices you now have with this business. It can make such a difference in your life and the lives of those you care about.

Think about what makes the other 5 percent so successful. Are they a million times smarter than the 95 percenters? Do they work a million more hours than anyone else? I don't think so. Many times all they did was seize the opportunity of the hour as you now have a chance to do with this business. Do what those in the 95 percent group *won't do*—set a goal, make a plan, and take action.

The success of the 5 percenters wasn't achieved instantaneously upon arrival at their chosen destination. They worked a period of time for it—perhaps years. Your success will take time too. It's a process. Your success begins the moment you make a decision to take advantage of the opportunity before you, and commit to doing whatever it takes to get there. Success is a journey, not a destination.

"Aspiring millionaires are best advised not to go to work for big corporations. In fact, 85% of America's millionaires own their own businesses...."

U.S. News & World Report

Chapter Three

Working With The Web Without Getting Tangled

"The Internet and e-commerce offer an exciting new opportunity for anyone to launch a big business from their home."

Stand Out By Standing Up

Each week hundreds of thousands of new sites appear on the World Wide Web. How are you going to get anyone to notice what you believe to be the greatest opportunity on the Internet? Especially when many of the websites out there are saying the same thing about their opportunity.

You first need to understand that this business is not about websites. It's about providing people with an opportunity to succeed. It's about developing into the person you've always wanted to be, and helping others do the same. It's about doing the work now and being paid for your efforts for the rest of your life.

The main website gives people an up to the minute glimpse of the possibilities and provides a convenient way to order products and services. That's what makes it an effective *tool*. But see it as a tool, not as the entire toolbox. Since it is only one of your tools, you will also need the others to get the job done. Keep your toolbox loaded with the latest tools so you can expedite your growth.

To be successful in the business, you need to make others aware of what it is, how it works, and what it could mean to them and their future. The website is a wonderful credibility builder. It can help fill in the blanks. Once people are in, it will also help them manage their businesses by providing up to the minute information. Building the personal relationships that really make this business go will be up to *you*.

Say you decide to create your own website (which is optional), in line with the business rules regarding this, of course. There are only three ways that people can get to your website. 1) Accidentally, while your site is still new, by searching the Web for the latest sites; 2) They can be brought there by someone else in your business, in which case they could join that person's business; or, 3) You can do what people have done to build this business since the very beginning; tell them about it, ask if they are looking to do more, and then take them to the site yourself.

You Can't Build A House With Just A Hammer

Building anything well, whether it's a successful business or a dream home, requires the right tools. Sometimes people put too much emphasis on tool selection and not on the task at hand. Having a favorite tool is comforting but no one tool will complete any large job. Just take the "tool box" with you so you're ready to meet almost anyone's particular needs.

Some tools, when added to your toolbox, will make a significant difference in the speed and quality with which you finish your work. But, of course, you need to understand and properly use the tools. When you correctly use a tool with confidence, that's when you'll realize the difference. Proper use of the main and/or your own website can help attract others to you and your opportunity.

If you develop a habit of relying too heavily on a particular tool, just the opposite can occur. You may begin to believe that nothing can happen without it, forgetting you're the main ingredient. You could lose confidence in your own ability to be successful through building your relationships with others. You may think that the tool is the only reason you've come this far. If that happens, people may actually shy away from you because you'll be operating on memory and habit rather than confidence, excitement, and a strong sense of what tool you can best use in any given situation.

It's sure easy to get excited about the Internet, but you also need to have confidence in the value of all the other tools in your box. One of the great things about this business is that people can still succeed without the use of a computer. In fact, they have for years. What that means is there could still be some people who might choose to build their business without getting involved with computers or the Web. Just be patient with them as they develop a better understanding of the potential. They may change their mind in time.

When you're confident and excited about this opportunity you can attract all types of people, both computer-oriented and not, and help them build a solid and profitable future. This can benefit you considerably as well. But, if you rely on only one tool, for example, the Web, you may not attract those less likely to go for the Web. They too can be a part of your business and still build a successful business. So you don't want get tangled-up, with or without the Web. As always, be flexible when approaching and working with people. It takes all kinds to build a successful business.

Keys, Food, Tools, And Methods

Imagine a series of doors. Behind each is an opportunity to share this business with a few people. Perhaps you have been looking behind the same doors for years with various degrees of success. When you get rejected at a particular door, you may find it harder to go back and open it again.

One day you're given a key to a brand new door. Behind it are people you've never been able to contact before. You're excited! You rush right past the other doors and burst into this new room full of people. What do you do now?

Suppose they were pigeons who hadn't eaten in a while. Imagine you had some food — enough to feed all of them for a long while. What do you think they'd do if you came at them running and shouting at the top of your lungs, "I've got the food you need! Come on over and I'll give you some"? How many of those pigeons do you suppose would use their last ounce of strength to fly away from you? All of them.

Now what do you suppose would happen if you got near them and gently sprinkled a bit of food around and waited? After they sampled it, you could sprinkle some more. Soon a trust would develop and I wouldn't be surprised a bit if some of them actually came over and ate out of your hand.

Same tool — different method.

Use the Internet and websites as new tools. As keys that unlock different doors. Approach it that way and you'll get the full benefit of its power. "Sprinkle samples around" until they're eating out of your hand.

The Internet Is An Exciting New Lever

You now have your hands on one of the most powerful opportunities on the planet. It gives anyone the ability to leverage his or her time and effort to build a solid and financially free future. Adding new technology to the business gives you a more powerful lever to excite and attract more people, enhancing your potential for growth.

Now you can share information with people around the country "in an instant." They no longer have to wait for anyone or anything else to see or learn about the latest innovation. The Internet can effectively allow you to be in several places at once. You can now share this information with many more people in a day than ever before.

However, you need to remember the key ingredient — again, it's *you*. The information you provide through the main website on the 'Net is certainly packaged in a wonderfully professional manner with lots of graphics, and it's easy to access. Looking at it will surely generate some curiosity and a desire to know more. That's where the most important ingredient comes in. This mix all starts and ends with the controller of the lever — you!

When you truly see yourself as the most important part of this equation, and don't take a back seat to the new technology, your confidence will grow. You'll feel more in control of the use of these great new tools and this mastery will carry over to those you contact and, in many cases, generate more interest. Those same people will sense your confidence and are more likely to find reasons to visit the website rather than search for excuses to avoid you.

Computers and the Internet are wonderful tools for you to use and control. Once again, this business is providing you with the latest and greatest tools for your success. Who knows what's next? All you can be sure of is that while the tools in the business will always be the best available, nonetheless, they're just tools — they're useless until you take action, share the business with other people, and give them an opportunity to use these great tools too. Again, the key to their success will be *themselves* — not the tools!

Chapter Four

Alphabet Soup For The Internet Soul

"You don't have to know how a computer or the Internet works in order to use them."

Can You Spell Gigabyte?

HTML, ISP, Java, Meta tags, scripts, bits, bytes, baud, servers, and the like. Each has an important function on the Internet and within each computer. How important is it for you to have a complete understanding of these terms and what they actually do to make this business work?

Let's look at this another way and ask some other questions. How important is it for you to understand the types of engines used in the trucks that deliver the products you have ordered? Will you be more or less successful once you understand why the distribution centers were placed where they were?

Knowing how things work seldom makes them work better. However, having confidence that many people with the right knowledge put this system together *is* very important. Knowing that a product, service, or opportunity can do what it's supposed to do, coupled with your confidence in the people who put it together, is far more important than understanding why every component was placed where it was or how it was all developed.

Does Anybody Know What Time It Is?

Did you ever ask for directions and it seemed like the person giving them to you was describing how the roads were built rather than how to get there? When things like that happen, we often don't hear the answer to our original question.

It's like going to the store to make a preplanned and very specific purchase. You can buy what you want at several places but chose one, in particular, for whatever reason. Upon arriving, you describe to the salesperson exactly what you came there to buy.

Without warning, they go into a long speech about the merits of your selection. Then they begin to educate you about each and every aspect of what goes into producing the item in question. But, you couldn't care less!

So, gradually, you lose interest in the purchase and your only concern is escaping from the situation as quickly as possible. When you do get out of there, you feel tense and angered at what was a very unpleasant situation. The salesperson can't understand you not wanting to know all about what you wanted and therefore considers you as a less than serious buyer. The bottom line is, neither of you got what you wanted.

You need to keep that in mind when offering this great opportunity to people. Some will want to get in the business immediately after seeing the website. Others will want more information, and still others will really want to investigate this whole concept before making a decision. Any one of those people, with obviously different personality types, could become a part of your business and achieve great success working with you. Given that each person has a sincere level of interest, the results you get are largely determined by how you treat them in the process.

When someone asks you what time it is,
don't tell them how to build a watch!

Take Them Where They Want To Go

The characteristics of your interest in this opportunity are as unique as you are. You bring your personal history, habits, personality, talents, skills, dreams, and goals as a part of what you have to offer as an individual. You know that achieving your objectives could make a positive difference in your life. The people who came before you, and those who can help you as you grow your business, want you to achieve your dreams and goals. Be grateful. In this busy workaday world, most people aren't interested in us enough to take the time to discover our dreams — or are even aware that we have them. Isn't it refreshing to have someone stop and ask you what your dream is?

The people who join you in this business may or may not care about your dream — or even know you have one. They have dreams of their own. Fulfilling those dreams is what drives them. Your greatest key to building a successful business is to do whatever it takes to help these people realize *their* dreams. Nothing less will work.

Most people you'll talk to about this opportunity will either be working for someone else in a job setting or working at a business of their own. In either case, they're generally directing almost all their efforts toward pleasing others — bosses or customers.

Trying to get them into the business because it will please you is probably the last thing any of them wants to do. They've got enough people to please at work and at home. They'd like to do something that really pleases them, especially if they dislike going to work, as 70 percent of people do. To them all you would have offered is another job to rob them of what little free time they have. No one wants to put out a lot of effort so they can someday sit back and look at what rewards you got from their work.

Find out what motivates *them*. What gets them excited? Then share with them how using the Internet and the other tools this business provides, along with your commitment to help them, can enable them to get where they want to be. Show them how people have helped you and why that makes such a powerful difference, when it comes to attaining success. Rather than tell them about your dream — focus on *their* dream. This may take some patience because they may have stuffed it away deep in their memory — believing it was just wishful thinking. Give them hope that it *can* happen for them.

Two To One — The Ratio That Pays

There's an old expression, "People don't care how much you know until they know how much you care." There are many areas of my life that have become more developed since becoming associated with this business, but by far the greatest accelerator to my success has been the ability to listen. When I made the needed improvements in that area, great things just seemed to happen. Once I experienced the power of being a good listener, it became my most effective skill for success. When you truly listen to what others are saying, that shows them you care.

Very few people will be "impressed" into this business. Most people, when they first learn about it and become interested, simply see something in it for themselves. (Look at people as having "WII-FM?" stamped on their foreheads — "What's In It For Me?") Showing them an impressive website, in and of itself, probably won't attract them to say "yes." However, sharing how that website can help them achieve the goals and dreams they told you about, *can be* powerful. That's the approach you may need to use — especially for those who are not technology-oriented.

Web or no Web, one of the best ways to demonstrate your sincerity and caring has always been to listen. When you first meet someone, use the 2 to 1 ratio. You have two ears and one mouth — listen twice as much as you talk! When you do, it's highly likely you'll hear exactly what you need to hear so you can share your business in a way that's attractive to them — in a way that fits their needs.

Of course, that still doesn't guarantee they'll say "Yes." Nothing absolutely guarantees that. However, what listening does do is gives you important information you can use to raise their curiosity to want to at least look at something that may address their financial concerns and how they can reach their goals and dreams. Caring about others, by listening to them, often helps them to be more inclined to look at what you have to offer. You can open the door to their believing that you could, at least, have a possible solution to things they'd like to change in their lives.

The bottom line is, they need to tell you what their concerns are. Are they not making enough money? Are they in danger of being laid off? Would they like to spend more time with the people they love? Are they worried about their retirement? These are all legitimate concerns, but in all my years as a businessperson, professional speaker and trainer, I've never been able to know they have them just by looking at the person the first time I met them.

How Can You Encourage Them To Talk?

One of the challenges in starting a conversation with someone you've just met, is encouraging them to talk — to really share what's on their minds and in their hearts. It's not very likely that they've been standing or sitting there, waiting for someone like you to come along to reveal their most pressing problems to. You're also not looking to start a counseling session. What you want to do is help them through what might be an awkward opening and let nature take its course.

After you've introduced yourself, ask them what they do for a living. Find something interesting about that line of work and comment on it. Ask them how long they've been doing it. Then see if they'll tell you whether they think it's the kind of work that provides long-term security. In this day and age, that could *really* get them going!

What will probably happen is they'll realize you've shown more interest in them than anyone else has in a long time. They'll relax and feel comfortable with you. It's also very probable that once they're done sharing they'll, in turn, ask you what you do — and that's where the "magic" can begin. What you say can either answer their question or open the floodgate to information that lets you know what would be interesting to them about your business.

"I work with people and help them set up successful businesses using the power of the Internet."

That statement says a tremendous amount about who you are and what you do. *"I work with people...."* Not a sell job. They begin to understand that whoever associates with you in your business will have help to *"...set up successful businesses...."* This phrase helps to eliminate any doubt of whether or not what you do is effective. You're telling them it already is.   *"...using the power of the Internet."*   This phrase lets them know that you're on the "cutting edge" — associated with the most talked about technology today. This adds to your credibility as well as that of the business.

That's still not the best part of making that statement, *"I work with people and help them set up successful businesses using the power of the Internet."* The great thing is, there is likely to be a definite response from your new "friend." That response allows you to go back to being a good listener and generally tells you what part of this opportunity they might be most interested in. The question they may well ask might be as simple as, "How do you do that?" Or they may tell you how they feel about the Internet. Better still, they may say something like, "The way things are going at work, I wish I knew something about that." That could be your "green light."

Use your imagination to see where this can go. The beauty of it is, if you let the person talking to you lead the way — by listening carefully, sharing appropriately, and asking questions, it's very likely you'll get to where you want to go with more than just yourself. If you're just looking at the business, the person who shared this book with you can give you even more ideas to help you "open the eyes" of those *you'd* like to share this business with. If you're already in the business, the leaders in your organization can do the same.

"No one's job is secure in the new economy, from the corporate chief executive to the ordinary worker."

Robert Reich, U.S. Secretary of Labor

Chapter Five

There's Plenty Of Room To Grow In Cyberspace

*"Remember when you were a kid and thought you could be
and do anything when you grew up? Start dreaming again
and surrender yourself to the possibilities."*

The One Percent Solution

Back in the 1960's, John Paul Getty was one of the richest
men in the world. Back then, he offered some sage advice
concerning his secrets for wealth. One is to have your own
business—85 percent of millionaires own their own
businesses. The second, and perhaps the most powerful
guidance Getty gave, is to *leverage* your time and effort with
others. He said, "I'd rather have the results of 1 percent of
the efforts of 100 men than 100 percent of my own."

If you're unable to work because you're sick or something
else happened, and you're all you've got, nothing can be

produced. Say you're leveraging with 100 people. That means that if half of them, 50, can't or don't work, the other half will still be producing something. However, in this business, leveraging alone, as powerful as it is, isn't the only ingredient that can help you become successful and financially secure.

If you have 100 people in your business and they're all unfocused, untrained, and going in several different directions, it's highly unlikely that their collective 1 percents of production will ever amount to much. Everyone needs to be moving in the same general direction, as a team. Your business can grow tremendously when you are highly productive and the people working with you duplicate your efforts and leverage their time and effort just as you're doing. In order for that to happen, everyone needs to be "on the same sheet of music."

Let's look at one of the best examples of leveraging in today's world. Close your eyes. Picture yourself at the counter of a McDonald's. Without opening your eyes, tell me where the fries are. Point to where they make the shakes. Where do the burgers go? Most everyone reading this lives in a different place and yet the (correct) answers are still the same. The fries are to the left, sodas to the right, and the burgers near the middle.

Now we all know how successful McDonald's is as a business. But, how many of you would say that they make the best hamburger you've ever tasted? Due to varied personal preferences, some of you will probably say "yes," while others may respond, "no." Yet, in spite of that, how would you explain the reason for them selling more burgers and fries in a day, than most restaurants sell in a lifetime?

They've *leveraged* their efforts and created *a system* of *duplication* that has proven to be effective in selling meals quickly. (They also cater to kids and attract them by the droves, usually with their parents' open wallets in hand!) No matter where you are in the world, when you — if you're an experienced McDonald's customer — enter through those Golden Arches, you know exactly what you're going to get.

The Secret Is Still The System — And Always Will Be

When I first looked at this business, I was confused. On one hand I was told that in order to succeed I needed to be willing to do things that were a bit different from my work. That made sense to me. Then they told me that if I simply duplicated what those who came before me did, I would succeed sooner. That's the part I didn't understand.

I used to be under the assumption that to be successful I needed to try to somehow get away from what I didn't want — which was always "settling for" what I had — instead of *driving toward* something I truly wanted. This, of course, was the result of doing what "everyone else" does. I learned that to be successful I needed to focus on and go toward my dream, rather than being pushed by my circumstances.

Long-term success in this business is a result of consistently and persistently following a successful pattern. It can be duplicated by anyone with the desire, drive, and discipline to carry it through to get the results they want. Unfortunately, many people are missing one or more of the above qualities and never see it through i.e., they quit on themselves. So, in the business, what may appear to be a massive group of people copying each other, is simply people duplicating a system of success — much like those who own McDonald's franchises do. Had people outside the business duplicated the principles of success that have existed for centuries, their lives, and the lives of those around them, would already be better.

I didn't understand that until the person who sponsored me first asked me this question: "John, if time and money were no object, what would you like to be doing in two to five years?" I must have looked like a puzzled pup, the way I felt my head tilted to one side, trying to come up with an answer to his question. Frankly, I hadn't been thinking much beyond that week's paycheck, let alone a few *years* down the road.

But, it was his next question that started to clear the fog in my mind. "If you're not looking specifically for anything more out of life, why do you think you'd be willing to work at anything extra?" Again, I had no answer. But I realized I had the makings of a challenge here. If I couldn't find a reason to get out of the situation I was in, what would be my purpose for doing anything different? I was temporarily stumped.

With his help, I began to start putting Johnny, the child, back into my mind and heart. You know, the young you who knew nothing of limits? The kid who could once imagine playing first base for their favorite big league baseball team or discovering new things for the benefit of the world? The young you who could rise above any limit set by an adult, just by closing your eyes and seeing it happen?

Then my friend shared the secret — the "hidden treasure" that could make anything I was willing to work for happen. The secret that made possibility thinking exciting for me again. He told me that if I was willing to simply imitate the activities of the people who had already succeeded at this business, and repeat the process over and over again, I could win. If I was willing to share what I had learned with enough people and help them get to where they wanted to be, I could have everything I could dream of. Wow!

The best part was, all this had been made into a simple system. A system that virtually anyone, with the ability to dream, could duplicate. A system that also provides you with caring mentors who are willing to support and guide you to your dreams. All for no extra charge. All they ask is that you be willing to pass what you've learned on to others. And the great thing is, this will cause you, as well as them, to grow.

The support system has many tools available, which you can purchase on an optional basis. There are audiotapes, which you can listen to at any time. These can educate as well as inspire you. Often people who came from backgrounds and had challenges similar to yours are recorded, as they speak at a seminar on how they climbed the staircase of success. By listening in your car, you can create a "university on wheels." This allows you to learn at your own pace, while utilizing that precious time to your advantage.

There are also positive books. You can read books written by and about people who have achieved success in their own lives. Some have success principles and inspiring stories, others may be biographies and human interest stories. All the books are selected based on their ability to enrich your life and continue your personal and business development.

You can also attend seminars and other functions. These events showcase the true heroes of this business. You get to listen to and meet people who have done what it takes to reach their goals. They have helped enough other people achieve the successes that they wanted, and, as a result, became successful themselves. These people tell their stories, and how they overcame their hardships. They also share business-building ideas to inspire and educate you and let you know that you can do it too.

Enter The Internet...

What's new and exciting is that you also now have the Internet at your disposal. It gives you virtually instant communications with the people who can help you, as well as with those you can help. Information about new products and services, as well as other messages can literally be sent to millions with the simple push of a button. Products can be ordered "on line," from the comfort of your home, and delivered right to your door.

But the real beauty of this system is that it's optional. That's right. As an independent businessperson, you make the choice. Above all else this is your business and no one can force you to use the Internet, the products, or the system of success if you don't want to. But remember what was said earlier about success being a simple path to follow. You can trace the steps of those who have gone before you or you can try to blaze new trails. You can go it alone the hard way, or choose to follow the lead of and have the help of others who've already made the trip. It's totally up to you.

Dare To Dream

It was just a few decades ago that technology gave us a way to talk to someone a great distance away, making them sound like they were in the same room. The telephone revolutionized business. But more than that, the *people* who saw the potential of the telephone and were willing to fail several times, as they attempted to best use it, were the ones who created the revolution. The phone is just a tool that people use. It can't do anything by itself. Without people it just sits there.

Then fax machines came along and enabled us to send whole documents around the world almost instantly. A new revolution? It's certainly a great electronic device. But, once again, the new revolutionaries are the people behind it, as well as those who creatively use it.

And now we have the Internet — an absolutely marvelous electronic dream come true. You can talk, write, send documents, or conduct business with thousands (or even millions) of people at the same time. Most marvel at that kind of power, but a new group of revolutionaries are exploding their businesses using this powerful tool. But again, it's the people who *use* the tool who build their success with it.

Another name for a revolutionary is a dreamer. A person who dares to dream opens their life to new possibilities. Whether it was with the phone, the fax, and now the power of the information superhighway, these dreamers see new technology as providing new tools that, when used properly, can change the lives of those who use them.

Every great accomplishment starts with a dream. The person who succeeds the most in life is the one who dreams big and takes action on their dreams. Those possibilities cannot become realities until you open your mind and let them in. *By dreaming you surrender yourself to the possible.* You position yourself on the side of "I can do it," rather than being fenced in by "It can't happen." You're the one who cuts "can't" out of your dictionary!

It's been said that all the world is a stage. You need to decide if you want to be in the play or just hang out in the audience. Having appeared on stage as a speaker and also having been in the audience, I can tell you this. The loudest applause, and the most hoots and hollers were for those who risked it all and got up on stage and told their story.

"Today, however, the great opportunities (for creating wealth) lie in distribution. In the past two decades, the majority of great personal fortunes have been made by people who found better ways of distributing things."

Success Magazine

Chapter Six

How <u>Not</u> To Get Caught In Traffic On The Information Superhighway

"Don't get caught up in the details. Focus on where you want to go and jump right in."

Getting Good Or Getting Going

Whether you've been building your own business for a long time just getting started, or still looking at the possibilities, using the technology of the Internet is exciting. Some of you may be saying to yourself that when you finally understand this and can get out there to tell people about it, your business will be awesome.

If you believe that, don't be shocked when someone you know gets in the business with someone else who can't tell the difference between a website and a spider web. Practicing never sponsored anyone. Until you're in front of a real live human being, you'll just be a well-rehearsed business of one (or two, if you have a spouse or someone else as a partner).

To my knowledge, no one has ever gotten in this business because someone rehearsed enough to pronounce all the words correctly and had all the facts in a neat and precise order, as they shared the business plan. Instead, it's more likely that they were excited and shared it with all their heart. They sincerely cared about the people they were sharing with and helped them discover their dreams. Everyone who understands this business and who's serious about building it big knows it is a people business built on empathy, emotion, enthusiasm, and dreams.

Caring about others, and sharing with sincere emotion how you feel about the business and the people who are helping you, are key to your success. This, along with your emotions, as you express yourself, will do more to attract others to associate with you than just getting all the facts right ever will. They will be buying into your concern for them, your enthusiasm, and their own potential—not "perfection" and accurate accounting.

Think about this. How many of your friends, upon hearing all the details in your serious fact-filled report about your involvement with the Internet, would be excited enough to ask you if there were any business opportunities for them with you? When you show them the technology and long-term growth forecasts, will they be begging to get in?

To put it more simply, how many of your friends like you because of how much you know? Do they associate with you because they know you have all the right answers and hang onto your every word? Probably not. Nor is it likely that you rehearse before each of their visits. You just act like yourself, right? One of the secrets of building a successful business is to build a friendship first, then build a business around it.

Perhaps you're worried about the fact that the technology of this business is changing so rapidly that you'll never be able to keep up with it. Well, don't fret; you don't have to! You can learn as you go along. Just go out and share this opportunity with others and the technology will take care of itself. Yes, technology is a wonderful tool, but it can't care about people. That's where you, the human element, come in. While the power of the Internet can be used to enhance your business, it can't build it for you by itself.

Even though most people you see may look good, sound good, and smell good on the surface, keep in mind that deep down inside they're all hurting to one degree or another. Everyone alive is dealing with some undesirable situation, circumstance, or challenge. And guess what? You can offer them a solution that can help them turn things around and put smiles on their faces.

For those of you who want to practice before you go out there and approach those on your list, here's a suggestion. It could help you make your presentations better and possibly help you build your business.

First, let's talk about the method of rehearsal. It's difficult, at best, to rehearse anything alone, especially in front of a mirror. You may want to do that for your first run through, just to get rolling. (Some do it in front of their cat or dog!) But doing it in front of other people is the best thing you can do. You need someone to point out where you can make adjustments, change the way you say certain things, and even show you where you need to be quiet and listen. But you don't want to risk a good prospect. So, who would you show it to?

Since most people begin building their businesses with a list, let's create a list of critics — people who will gladly critique your approach and presentation. They will be brutally honest, and tell you everything you did wrong. And who knows? They may get excited and want to associate with you and your opportunity anyway. Regardless of what they say or do though, they will have absolutely no effect on your prospect list because they aren't even on it!

Now get a pen and paper. Without thinking or analyzing, write down the names of everyone you can think of who will never be interested in anything you have to say. These are the one's you've determined that would *never* be interested in anything like this.

That's who you can practice on. Every new technique. Every improvement in your business. Every time you feel a little stale in your approach. And, now that you've got the technology of the Internet in your toolbox, you may even want to go back and "practice" on everyone who's already said they weren't interested before the Internet was a part of your business.

The reality is, you need to practice by doing. Working with real people and having a real experience are really the only ways to improve. Doing anything else will give you little, if any, results. You need to risk mistakes and possible rejection before you can ever hope to succeed. (Otherwise you'll end up with a great fact-filled presentation that is only presentable to the mirror, the dog, or the cat)! So be excited and go out and share the business. Forget about being perfect at it. Just care about others and show them how they can have a better life too. If you should stumble a little, you'll be more relatable anyway. So just have fun with it.

Attitude, Attitude, Attitude

One of the best things you can do to attract people is with your positive attitude. An upbeat forward-thinking, and confident attitude, or a limited and downtrodden attitude, can affect an entire room of people.

How many of you have heard about having a positive attitude? Are you sick of it? How many of you actually have a negative attitude toward having a positive attitude? I understand — I once spent a lot of money buying all those attitude programs that are out there. But, they didn't work. Why? Simply because I didn't understand the power of my attitude. Had I understood, you can bet I'd have paid closer attention and had more success sooner!

The reality is that having a positive mental attitude does work. It not only works, but is key to your success in this business or in anything else in life. It can and does change an entire room when you walk into it. A "room's attitude" is the average of everyone's attitude in the room at a given time. For example; let's say a "one" is a negative attitude and a "ten" is a positive attitude, and by your walking into a room it can change. Suppose you went to work and nine people were in the coffee room and everyone had a "one" for attitude. All they were doing is their typical gossiping, whining, and complaining. You enter on top of the world and you're a "ten." If you add up everyone's attitude and take an average, the room's attitude went from a "one" to a "two." So, just by walking into the room *you* doubled the room's positive attitude.

Now you might be thinking, "Maybe it would be better if I didn't go into the coffee room because the negative attitudes filling the room could negatively affect me." You're right! It's smart to associate with positive-thinking people as much as possible. You want to fill your mind with positive ideas as much as you can. Also, listening to positive tapes and reading positive books helps you to replace any negative thoughts you may have with dream- achieving positive ideas.

A great attitude helps you gain confidence. That's the key you need to unlock and develop big dreams. A positive attitude changes those "wishful thinking" ideas into real possibilities. It helps you focus on the possibilities rather than the challenges. If things don't go as well as you had planned, your confidence—and most importantly your dreams—will help you stay motivated to keep on going. And that may be all you need to make your dreams come true — that extra boost. Once you discover the power of a positive attitude, you'll feel weak without it and will do whatever it takes to get it back. As the old saying goes, *"It's your attitude and not your aptitude that determines your altitude in life."*

"Crowd Followers" And "Dream Reachers"

In this business, you need to focus on your dream—not on the details. People who are constantly researching details to get all the facts, afraid of making a mistake, often pass by the joys of life without even realizing it. These folks tend to follow the crowd. They do it blindly, never looking around to see if there are any other options.

Here's a little story that really proves the point. It's about a trip I take to New York City by traveling Route 95.

As you enter the state of New York on 95 South, you approach a row of tollbooths. This is one of the widest strips of tollbooths I have ever seen. There are lanes everywhere to choose from so that you can pay to continue your journey. Almost every time I approach them I notice quite a few lanes that are backed up. I also observe that there are one or two lanes that are wide open that no one is using.

I shift over and get into one of the open lanes, pay the toll, and I'm on my way. Makes sense, right? Yet time and time again, I see people changing lanes to get into the crowded ones. Why? I guess they think they'll be missing something. The "crowd followers" generally focus on what's right in front of them—they tend to follow the crowd. Whereas, "dream reachers" stay focused on the destination they're heading toward and look for the best way to get there.

"Life is a highway. The enjoyment you get
depends on the lane you choose. "

Focusing on your destination is the easiest and, in fact, the only way to get there. When you keep in mind where you're going, you see the bigger picture and the potholes and detours along the way fade into oblivion. Dream reachers realize that each step brings them closer to where they want to be and, as they get nearer, they actually get stronger and more resolved about reaching their dream or goal.

The difference between a crowd follower and a dream reacher is simple — *it's a decision.* That's all. Anyone who wants to start succeeding can begin, simply by deciding to do so. Not getting hung up on minor details, and focusing on what you believe is your ultimate goal, will make you a true dream reacher.

Anything worth having is worth working for. The crowd follower is used to instant gratification. They focus on getting paid today for what they do today. The dream reacher is only interested in the ultimate payday. That's the one that will take care of him and those around him in ways a crowd follower can't even comprehend.

The expression, "There's safety in numbers," was not meant for dreamers. I think it applies to antelopes on the lion-infested plains of Africa, but not to people. Most of us have certain fears about death and dying. Mine is to die in insignificance. I want to make a difference in as many people's lives as I can. How about you? Dream reachers make a difference.

Are You A Rubbernecker?

I grew up just outside of New York City. Every day you'd hear where the traffic jams were and how long people would be delayed getting to and from work.   Many times, amazingly, what caused a traffic jam was not what you might think.

Often, it wasn't the breakdown of a car or even an accident. It was people slowing down just to see what was going on! They felt they needed to take in the entire situation — perhaps to figure out the details. In any case, if you were near them or behind them, you were going to be stuck in traffic because of them.

Every day the same places seemed to be backed up. Those who truly wanted to get to their destinations would make alternate plans. Leave a little earlier or later. Go a different way. Their positive possibility thinking attitude kept them focused on their destination. They always look for better ways to arrive and are willing to risk taking different routes.

I guess that's what makes the dream reacher—the leader—so unique. More people are too busy following the other crowd followers than are willing to take a chance. That's too bad because success is a wonderful journey that everyone can take. All they need to do is look ahead and focus on where they want to go.

Don't get hung up just watching all the wonderful changes that technology is bringing to this business. Use the "ready, fire, aim" approach. Go with what you've got when you've got it. Take what you have and go out and share it with as many people as possible.

The new things that get developed down the road will benefit those most who are using what already exists to the best of their ability. Pick your own fast lane! Don't dwell on the problems and challenges in your life. Fix your eyes on your dream, and become a vital part of the solutions this business is providing.

Take Action With A Purpose

Why do you do what you do? Ask that of most people and they'll probably reply that they "have to." They need their job to pay the bills. They work for someone else, because that's what they believe they're supposed to do.

Taking care of your needs today is important. But what about tomorrow? How do you know what the future will bring unless you've taken steps to ensure that what you want will be there when you need it? Have you ever thought about the possibility of something happening to you that could prevent those things from occurring?

If you're relying on the plans of others, i.e., your employer or someone else for your future, who's in control? The fact is, most people will change careers three times and work an average of ten jobs before they're 65. How do you build a pension with any company when you're not there long enough?

If you want to run a business, don't imitate the local candy store. Do what the big corporations do—diversify. While you're earning a paycheck, use the power of the Internet to help you share this great business with others. Create a long-term residual income that can be yours, regardless of what type of pension you may or may not have.

Get out of the traffic jam of ordinary life and take the fast lane to where you want to go. You can get there sooner and avoid the chance of a major accident. It seems as though there are fewer people on the road to success, just in case you hadn't noticed!

"If you could create a monthly residual income of $3,000, that would be the equivalent of having nearly $900,000 in the bank paying you interest."

Chapter Seven

The Most Important Ingredient

"People using technology to move ahead can get there sooner."

Everybody's New And Improved

Just because someone or some advertisement says something is better, doesn't necessarily mean it is. Its success or lack thereof is based on the most powerful marketing force in the world — *word of mouth.* What are large groups of people saying about this or that? Are they excited? Are they skeptical? Are they using it themselves?

This business has always been an opportunity that is second to none. The additional enhancement via the Internet simply demonstrates the willingness of the corporate suppliers and leaders in this business to seize opportunities — to help you to be more successful by providing you with a new effective tool.

Your use of the Internet is totally up to you. Rest assured that it has been researched and tested to the maximum level. It will do what it claims to do *when you do what you need to do.* And you need to expose this opportunity to as many people as possible and share the power of the Internet and how it could mean a better future for them.

Your business grows or sits idle depending on only one thing—*you.* You're the one who needs to launch it and create a solid foundation for it to grow and flourish. Will you do whatever it takes to make you and your business attractive to others? Just knowing how to do something the best way has never gotten it done. Understanding and committing to "WHY" you're doing it is what can create mansions out of dirt mounds, miracles out of maybes, and triumph out of turmoil.

Most people can understand what they would need to do with an opportunity to get where they want to in life. Unfortunately, many of them won't make the consistent effort needed to make it happen. The "how" is there but the dream—the reason to do what needs to be done—is often missing. Perhaps it is just hidden under years of complacency and not believing it could ever really happen for them, or that it's "pie in the sky"— unrealistic. The great thing is, you now have the opportunity to re-awaken a lot of people's dreams (including your own, if necessary) in a very exciting way. Dreams are the fuel in this business.

There are people in this business who have had tremendous success. Some of them will tell you that the reason they were able to succeed is because someone just like you thought enough of them to believe in them and tell them they could do it. Some of them tell the story about their humble start and say it was the first time in their lives someone really believed in them and helped them achieve their dreams. Your compassion for and confidence in another person, coupled with the power of the Internet, can be a very powerful combination.

You Need To Make The First "Investment"

Suppose you wanted to start a conventional business. You'd need at least one product or service, support materials, a place to conduct business, and perhaps a few other things. The most important resource you would need to get started would be money. But, if you don't have it, where would you go?

More than likely you'd approach a bank for a loan. But before they would even pull out an application to process it, there are a few things they'll probably want to know. Things like, did you refinance the mortgage on your home, cash in your life insurance, sell any stocks and bonds, or anything else that could raise capital? They'd be asking basically, "What have *you* put into the venture?"

If you've already made a substantial investment, they're more likely to be interested enough to go to the next step. Essentially, your initial personal investment would have attracted another potential investor — the bank. As long as they feel you've invested enough in an idea you believe in, they're more willing to consider investing and risking with you. If you're willing to protect (and build on) what money you've already put into it, the bank may decide it's safe to assume their investment would be protected as well.

If you were selling your home and *invested* in landscaping or a fresh coat of paint, you'd probably attract more buyers than if you didn't. A dirty automobile for sale doesn't attract as many customers as one who's owner invested in a good cleaning. Good investments can attract additional investors.

In the previous examples, *you* invested in your business *first* and *then* attracted others who invested later. The powerful fact is that successful results occur much faster when you have others investing in your idea. Outside "investors" are essential for long-term growth and success.

Now, you may have never started a conventional business, and you didn't read this far to learn how to sell your home or car, did you? So, you may be asking, "How does this apply to being an independent businessperson?" It's simply that you need to *invest in yourself.* And in the process, you need to understand a little bit about nature.

Everything on this planet that is alive and growing, does so from the inside out. The intake of nutrients creates growth from within that develops into expansion on the outside. When we take in the right foods on our way to becoming adults, we can enjoy healthy growth. However, go on a Rocky Road ice cream and chocolate diet and watch what happens. Our intake often determines our "outlook."

Now let's look at the human factor. Each of us has an ability to reason and dream. What kind of "nourishment" do we need to keep doing that? We need to feed our attitude. Yes, you can nourish yourself into having a positive attitude.

As we discussed earlier, continuing education-type things recommended by the leaders in your business can bolster your attitude. We're talking about things like books, tapes and seminars to help you grow. "But," you may be asking, "Is it really worth my while to spend time and money on my attitude?" Consider this. How can you expect someone else (the people who are helping you) to be willing to invest in your success and development if you aren't willing to do so yourself? If you don't want your dream or goal enough to invest in yourself, why should anyone else?

What's An Investment?

Perhaps the term investment is a little scary for you. You may see it as something that only successful and wealthy people are able to do. Let's see if this definition helps. *An investment is made up of small contributions over a sustained period of time that produce a yield greater than the sum total of all the contributions.* Not many people invest something one day and withdraw the next. Investing in yourself—in your attitude and skill level—is a process that makes you stronger and more attractive to others the longer you do it.

The first step is to target what types of investments in yourself will pay the highest dividends. First we have the positive books and tapes approved by your leadership. Tapes for travel in the car and the other times when you're doing something else — perhaps walking, working around the house, and getting ready for work or bed. Books are for other times — breaks and lunch at work or at home. Do you know that if you read just 15 minutes a day, over the course of your lifetime you'll have read enough to attain the equivalent of five college educations? Always carry a book to read when you have a few minutes to wait for something, like an appointment at a doctor's office. The average person in the U.S. reads only one book a year. Imagine how much more you'll be able to do when you read a new book every month!

Seminars are another investment you can make in yourself. There are seminars where you spend a day listening to people who came from where you are and have arrived at where you want to go. Here you can get inspired to activate yourself, learn what you need to avoid mistakes that have already been made, and what to do to maximize the results of your efforts. And you're hearing it all from people who are not just talking theory. They actually did it. They made the mistakes and developed the strength to see it through. The other thing is you'll be sitting with people who have dreams and goals just like you do. That's quite a support system for a very small investment of time and money.

Once you realize that there is no one or nothing on earth more worthwhile investing in than you are, you'll take the first step. Shortly after you begin that journey, you may be surprised at how many people will come into your life who will help you get where you want to go.

Nothing Works! — Nothing, That Is, Except People — And It All Starts With *You*

What have you got your hands on? Taking a look at everything here and considering the possibilities can sure get you excited. It's almost a can't-miss opportunity — a no brainer! However, there is a lot more information available than I can cover in this book — and that's where your leaders come in. Yet, by itself, information has no power. We all need to apply what we learn in order to be successful.

You've got the backing of one of the most respected companies on the planet. They have teamed up with hundreds of other highly reputable companies offering thousands of products with an unconditional, money-back guarantee. Despite that fact, these companies can't help you without *your* involvement, drive, and ambition.

They've gotten together to create the greatest Web opportunity ever known. You'll be able to reach any number of people "in an instant." They can be customers, members, or other independent business owners like yourself. You'll be able to monitor your own business's growth and activity anytime, anywhere, and up to the minute. But *you're the one* who needs to take the necessary steps to get the information.

The support system can provide you with materials such as books, tapes, CD-Roms, and literature. Schedules feature training sessions, seminars, conventions, leadership-sponsored events, and other valuable information and updates. At the seminars and conventions you can learn, grow, and celebrate the success you and others have achieved. You can plug everyone in your business into what the system offers. You can also find mentors who will work with, encourage, and guide you to whatever level you desire.

But simply finding out who these mentors are will not give you their knowledge. Tie yourself in tightly with these leaders and learn as much as possible from them. You need to promote the system and all it has to offer your people. While it's certainly true that it's optional — nonetheless, it's one of the key ingredients to being successful in this business — following the system of success.

It would be hard to look at all this information and not think this is a sure thing. It's hard to see how you could fail with all this going for you. Yet, if this were a cake to be baked, the most important ingredient would be missing.

To discover the missing ingredient, you'll need to check the recipe. Even after baking a few cakes, you'd probably still need to refresh your memory every now and again. The key to all of this, the one absolutely essential ingredient to your success, is waiting for you — right in the mirror.

Without *you*, none of this works. In fact, nothing works! Nothing, that is, except people — and it all starts with *you*. You need to be the driving force behind the growth of your business. You are the one who puts this information into the hands of those who are looking for a chance. If that doesn't happen, all of this wonderful technology and the opportunity stays a "secret." And keeping this a secret not only slows your growth, it also denies people you know and meet of an opportunity that can change their lives.

Make no mistake about it. You are the most important ingredient for your own success. The greatest investment in the world is *you*. Once you have a solid handle on your dream and the burning desire to achieve it, you'll find yourself willing to do whatever it takes to get there. That's when others will almost "magically" appear to help you on your way. This is because your commitment attracts others into your life to help you achieve your dream. Your own investment in yourself has a virtually limitless potential return. You are well worth investing in!

"The Internet is exploding. You can take action and it will propel you. Or, you can do nothing and get blown away with the dust left by others who are passing you by."

Chapter Eight

You CAN Lead

"The power of the Internet is awesome. Couple it with the power of setting an excellent example for others to follow and you could have great results."

Leaders Don't Grow On Trees

Suppose you can't tell the difference between a search engine and a searchlight. What if megabytes are something you thought described how to quickly eat a sandwich? The amount of knowledge you have right now about the Internet has little to do with the amount of success you can have. You can learn to be a leader as you go by asking for some initial instruction if you need to, learning as you do it, and asking for help as you go along.

Since leaders aren't wearing uniforms or nametags that say "LEADER," how would you know when you've found one? First you need to understand that knowledge and experience don't necessarily make a good leader. A true leader is the first to admit they don't know everything — they are humble.   One of the qualities that makes them a leader is that they care enough about other people to admit they need to ask someone else for help.   They want their people to get what they need to succeed. And they'll do whatever is necessary to make that happen.

Attracting leaders is the key to growing your business and improving your life, as well as the lives of those with whom you associate. Finding them quickly, introducing them to the system, and helping them get plugged into it can accelerate the growth of your business.   Hanging around with the leaders who have been in this business for a while will give you an education that no amount of college can. Soak up everything you can learn from them to build your business.

Becoming A Leadership Magnet

Building any type of business to a successful level requires people with leadership skills.   When you decide to build your business quickly, you need to load up with leaders who can and want to duplicate your efforts and enthusiasm. How can you find them? Better still, once you do find them, why would they want to work with you?

Are they attracted to you because you say things like the following?

"I don't like reading. Never did. Don't have much use for books anyway."

"I'm too busy to attend seminars but you should go. You're new."

"Call me as soon as you're ready to start having meetings. Then I can help."

"I'm not interested in that Internet stuff, and I didn't think you would be either."

Would you bet your chances of success on someone who makes those types of negative comments? In a business built on the principles of duplication, is that what you'd want others in your group to duplicate? They wouldn't get very far in the business, would they? I know that you wouldn't be making such "de-motivating" comments. If you thought that way, you probably wouldn't even be reading this book — or any other positive book for that matter. I pointed out these negative attitudes for you to keep in mind for the future. This is to help you be more aware of what you may be saying so you are positively influencing your people and others you associate with. One of the cardinal rules of the business is to always be positive with your people and other business associates.

Your future is not only going to be shaped by this new technology, but also by one of the oldest truths of success. It will be largely shaped by the books you read and *the people you associate with*. If you hang around negative-thinking people, you'll get negative results. If you hang around positive people and duplicate their attitudes, you're more likely to get positive results.

Help your people learn to be positive around their people and other associates, and to pass on this principle. They may themselves talk and act like the previous examples or run into people who do. Leadership can also be advising people what *not* to say or do. That can be just as valuable, if not more so, especially in some cases! Do only what you want duplicated!

Another way to recognize good leaders is by their service. Good leaders are great servers. They don't just dictate to their people. Instead, they share methodology and lead by example. They demonstrate the value of what needs to be done for growth by doing it themselves, in front of their people, as well as for their prospects.

Getting The Kids To Listen

How many of you who are parents tend to get frustrated around the fifth time (or maybe earlier!) that you have to repeat yourself to your kids? After 12 attempts at getting them to do their chores or clean their rooms, do you have any hair left to pull? Do you understand their secret language when they say things like, "Yeah I know," or "I did clean my room," just to get you "off their backs"? There *is* a solution.

Somewhere out there is likely to be a neighbor, relative, or other friend or acquaintance who thinks your kids are angels. You probably know who I mean. There can only be two possible reasons for their perception. First, these people have a distorted view of what is or isn't angelic. Or, more than likely, your kids really behave well in front of them.

If you determine that these people have a full understanding of reality, your solution may be to let them know what you'd like your kids to do and ask *them* to deliver the message. Perhaps your kids will listen to *them!* Most kids are image conscious and will go to great lengths to maintain appearances. This means you can get done what you want, lessen your frustrations, and have kids you can be even more proud of.

When you're willing to pass the credit on to someone else, your objectives can often be met. What difference does it make as to *why* they cleaned up their room or did their chores? You wanted those things done, you didn't want to fight about it, and now they're done. That's the positive result.

So what does all of this have to do with leadership and building this business? To build a successful business and to be an equally successful leader — *everything*. Becoming a professional in the business is a lot like being a parent. You need to realize there are certain things you do better than anyone and there are other things you don't do very well. Yet, you still need to get everything done. Often, the difference between an amateur and a professional in anything is that the professional knows when to get help. They've learned that it's better to wait for a more complete and accurate answer from a more experienced person. They don't blurt out the first answer, right or wrong, they can think of just to sound as though they know what they're talking about.

Great leaders know when to follow. They realize the benefit of getting a leader to speak, train, or counsel — someone who has had more success in a particular area. They're smart enough to ask that person to teach their people. Successful people in this business seek the help and counsel of their leader(s) who are willing to mentor them and share what they've learned in overcoming certain obstacles — as well as assist you in mapping out an action plan. These valuable sessions can shorten the time it takes you to reach the level of success you desire. Be humble and teachable. It works!

The Qualities Of An Excellent Leader

If you wanted to find an ideal leader, to be one of your associates, at the (fictional!) "Leader Store," you'd probably make a list of qualities you'd want this person to have. This way you'd be able to find one that will be exactly what you're looking for. We already know that one of the qualities of fine leaders is a service-oriented attitude toward those around them. But what other traits would you look for?

How about enthusiasm for the business, the great e-commerce potential, the products and services, the tools, and the people in the business? You'd certainly want someone who would follow the system and could teach it to others.

They'd be reading the recommended books, listening to the tapes, attending the functions and other leadership-sponsored events, and counseling with their mentor — to stay motivated, learn the latest information and approaches, and to get individual assistance.

Another important ingredient of an excellent leader is their willingness to share the dream with those around them. They need to care enough about others so that they do their best to "wake them up" to pursue their own dreams and goals. Then they focus on the goals and dreams of their people and how they could best support their people in accomplishing them, step by step. They would reserve talking about their own dreams and goals to when they're sharing with their leader or mentor who they go to for counseling.

The key to attracting leaders into your organization is simple. You need to become a leader yourself! People will tend to do what you do—not what you say. Follow the system and as your people duplicate what you do, they can become leaders in the business too.

Even if you're brand new to the business, you can still be a leader. Reread what an excellent leader does, as we just covered. See which of these things you may already be doing and what you may need to be doing. See. You're probably on your way to being a fine leader yourself, i.e., if you aren't one already!

Remember, people will tend to do what you do, not what you say. It's only by your example that you lead. Be the kind of person that you would like to have in your business. Do the things that you'd like your people to do. A leader never expects someone they are leading to do something they wouldn't do themselves.

There may be leadership qualities you feel you don't have or things you're not doing as well as you'd like, or even some things that you may not be doing at all. If so, ask your leader or mentor for some guidance. They can help you fine-tune. As you talk to your mentor, you can observe what an excellent leader does to help their people. Asking your leader for help will show those you've sponsored how important *their* leaders are to the growth of their businesses.

As you develop and demonstrate your skills as a leader, others will want to follow in your footsteps. And this will happen even more so when they see how your business is growing. Your actions will do more to attract leaders to you than all the mere looking for potential or actual leaders ever will. You need to know however, that the very moment you decide to become a leader, you've succeeded in the first step—making the decision. You can start to attract all the leaders and potential leaders you need into your business as soon as you start becoming one. Simply do all of the things that fine leaders do, and improve as you go.

Leadership is a process. Be patient with it. Both having your own independent business and leadership are not about finding other people or things to make you successful. They are about doing whatever it takes to develop yourself as a better person so *you* can help other people become the best they can be too. As they grow, following the system and building their businesses, your success will come, as a result.

You can move the process along faster by following the example of those leaders you most admire. You'll hear about or see them listen to certain continuing education and dreambuilding tapes over and over again. Do the same. When you watch them or hear about them helping their people build their businesses, do the same for your people. Once you begin imitating the qualities you admire, you'll see results. Upon seeing results, repeat the process. Repetition creates habits and, before you know it, the qualities you've been admiring in others become the same qualities that others are admiring in you.

Most businesses, to one degree or another, are built through the process of duplication. Why? Because the leaders find what works and go with it. In this business, though, the duplication benefits you as the independent business owner, rather than only benefiting the boss in a conventional business. You can develop the necessary leadership skills from duplicating of the skills learned from the leaders you respect. Those same skills will be duplicated by those you've sponsored who aspire to be leaders. It's people copying people who are plugged into the system. Leaders serving others, who are serving others, and on down the line. People helping people help people. And remember, the greatest leaders are the greatest servers!

The Difference Between Perfection And Excellence

Sometimes new people get frustrated if they can't seem to master one part of the business or another. They want to wait until they've practiced over and over, finally get it right, and then go out there and *try* it.

Trying is lying. Don't believe me? Take a break for a moment. Get a pen or a pencil and place it right in front of you. Look at it and concentrate. Focus your energy toward it. Now, *try* to pick it up. You can't. You either picked it up or you didn't. There is no try. *There is only the choice of doing or not doing.*

This business isn't perfect. Nothing is perfect and neither is anyone. Regardless of how big a business someone has, they're never perfect. Did you ever hear the expression that "nobody's perfect"? Is that a fact or just an excuse we sometimes hear when someone makes a mistake? The answer is, both are true. And as leaders you need to understand this. Leaders and leadership have nothing to do with perfection.   But they have everything to do with excellence.

Excellence And Leadership

What is excellence?   To me, excellence is —"doing as well as you can with the information at hand, using the experience you've gained since you've started, and asking for help as you need it." Excellence means you are constantly doing and growing. There is no status quo. With each task you undertake, you gain more knowledge and experience. That means the presentation of this business doesn't have to be perfect. Not even close. People want to see your passion and your level of commitment, not your grammar, math, or computer skills.

This is where true leaders have the opportunity to shine. Everybody wants to succeed — so why don't they? Plain and simple — it's probably their fear of failure. Leaders are willing to do something even if there's a possibility of failure. If they weren't willing to risk failure, they wouldn't do much, would they? Go back and reread the definition of excellence. Nowhere does it mention the word perfect or any other end result of an effort.   It's only based on putting everything you've got into what you're doing and the results "just happen," as a matter of course. You can't directly control the results—just the level of effort you put into getting them.

True leaders don't tell people what to do — they don't boss others around. They simply teach them what to do and show them by example.   That opens the door for two possibilities — success and failure.   Both are winners. If a leader is successful and a prospect gets "in," that demonstrates it can be done. However, it may be that a more valuable lesson is learned if they don't get "in." That leader demonstrates the possibility that even if you do everything "right," there are still no guarantees. When you're dealing with the human element, unpredictability can easily pop into the equation, as you may have noticed in the past!

Part of becoming a leader means searching inside for your own level of excellence and fine-tuning what you find. Succeeding as a leader means searching inside of others for their level of excellence, which may be hidden to them, and helping them bring it out and develop it to their full potential. *Always look at people as they can be, not as they are.* Oftentimes, leadership needs to be encouraged and developed over a period of time, just to get them "up and running." But true leaders are patient. Leadership is truly a journey toward excellence. And you need to include as many people to join you on that journey as possible. As each person reaches their own level of excellence and helps others do the same, your business will become that much stronger.

If You're Willing To Go It Alone — You Won't Have To After All

When your leader recommends something, the best way to promote it to your people is to be the first in line to participate. That is the only way you can reasonably expect your people to follow you. "Do as I say, not as I do," does *not* apply to leaders! Many have found a couple good people and then waited for their people to make them rich — only to learn that they won't. This attitude will only encourage duplication of itself throughout your business — which means everyone sits back and waits, and no one does anything! Your sincerity and consistent action, following the system and teaching others to do the same, and the friendships you build in the process, are what will build your business. And you build your credibility by "walking the walk," not by just "talking the talk"!

When you start to see successful results from your efforts, those with big dreams are more likely to want to follow in your footsteps, and take on a leadership role. After all, true leadership is taken — not given. As this happens, their leadership skills will become more evident to you and they'll really start to grow and develop as they persist in building the business. Others may have seen the leadership qualities in you and that's what may have attracted them to you. Some may take a bit longer to grow. Maybe they need to build a bigger dream to get them more excited. As they pursue that dream, they can blossom into leaders. The bottom line is you know you're being an effective leader when you see your people growing and duplicating your efforts!

When a true leader is so committed that they are willing and glad to do every aspect of this business on their own, it can be shortly after that realization that they no longer have to. Other budding leaders may already be starting to duplicate them and giving it all they've got. Here's a little slogan which sums up the attitude you need to have as a leader — *Believe in everyone, but count on no one.* The power of the Internet is awesome. Couple it with the power of setting an excellent example for others to follow, and you could have great results.

*"Being on the
right track without
taking action
just means
you'll get hit by
the train."*

Chapter Nine

In This Test
Copying Is Allowed

"The best way to succeed at anything is to duplicate what someone did who is already where you want to be. The system is a wonderful tool to support you in doing that."

What You Do Speaks So Loudly I Can't Hear What You're Saying

This is a business built upon the efforts of many leaders. When you have more than one leader the only way for you to participate in the massive growth that this business is experiencing, because of the Internet-based opportunity, is to have everyone following the system. Listening and duplicating may not be the same thing because people often interpret the same things differently. Observing what a leader does and then duplicating it is more likely to be effective because less is left to the imagination.

If you read someone the Declaration of Independence one time, it's highly unlikely they could repeat it back from memory. But if you took action and made copies, everyone you gave one to could read it out loud just as you did. It's never important for anyone to mechanically memorize what you do because in practice they'll be stilted and robotic. But it is very important for them to get a good sense of it and be able to copy what you do, incorporating their own unique qualities into what they're copying, i.e., personalizing it.

The greatest teacher sets an example by taking action. For example, if you know little about accessing and using the Internet and the business's Web page, it's likely some of your people have the same situation. So you could set an example by reading, listening to, and watching all the information available from the corporate supplier and your leadership organization, and encourage your people to do the same. You could also talk to your leaders about the possibility of having someone well-versed on the Internet do a training session for you and your people to teach some basics. This will be fun and will help reduce any fear of the unknown that you and your people may have.

Teaching by showing is far better than just telling people what needs to be done. The demonstration *shows* how it can be done — giving people a chance to see and hear it. And though mistakes may be made as you're demonstrating it, these, too, can be valuable lessons, and you may still achieve the necessary results. Another benefit is, even if you don't get the results you want, as you're practicing, you'll learn what not to do. With the teaching tools of example and demonstration, you and your people have a much better chance of learning what you need to do.

Failing can also be an awesome motivator. Say you're sharing the business with one or more prospects. When you are willing to fail — fumble around, or perhaps get something out of order — in front of others, you're exhibiting two important qualities. First, your willingness to goof up demonstrates that failing along the way is just part of the success process. It also shows them that it's more important to get out there and get going after your dream, than to sit home trying to get good at a presentation.

The second point failing demonstrates is that you don't have to be perfect to be successful. In fact, no one can be perfect. Your goal needs to be to show others that if you can do this, anyone can. This is true for learning the ins and outs of the Internet and everything else you do in the business.

Won't They Duplicate Your Failure?

Some people hold back from taking action in front of others so they won't be seen as failing. They fear that if they fail in front of an audience, that audience might repeat the failure. Let's hope they do!

Say you share this opportunity and every other beneficial aspect of this business with someone who says "no." Chances are, that person wasn't ready, didn't understand, was already headed in a different direction, or perhaps wasn't motivated enough to move on. This is not a failure on your part. The mere fact that you had an audience tells you that you did something right. The key to growth is to finish the lesson. Remember—*everybody's behavior is about themselves*. What people do or don't do is simply a reflection of where they are in life. Who knows, they may come your way later on as they see you grow or something changes in their life. A "no" may just be a "not now." Everyone in business gets "noes"!

Sharing this business is not about the answers you get along the way. It's about sharing the opportunity, regardless of the answers. If you fail to sponsor someone, and that's bound to happen, it is important to "pick yourself up, dust yourself off" and get back out there as soon as you can and share the business again. That's what you want your people to do. Right? Then *you* need to be the excellent example for them to duplicate!

Your example of going through the "noes" to get to the "yesses," will demonstrate an important aspect of this business. Leaders, and aspiring leaders, need to risk failure in order to have any chance at all to succeed. They need to be willing to face possible rejection and "weed out" the "noes" so they can sponsor the "yesses." Makes sense, doesn't it?

Also, it demonstrates that regardless of your level of experience, you are never going to be guaranteed a positive answer just because you show up and do a great presentation. That also means that someone could say "yes" even if you make mistakes with it, as well. The bottom line is that, if you're willing to open yourself up to the possibility of being turned down, you also expose yourself to the possibility of sponsoring someone! Know that it is anybody's guess what people are going to do as a result of your sharing this opportunity with them. This is just part of the reality of doing business. It's not unique to this opportunity.

Every successful leader in this business knows that if you share it with enough people, you may never have to work for anyone else ever again. (This assumes you're following the system, you're doing your best to plug the "yesses" into it, and that they duplicate you.) Sharing is one of the most important ideas to keep in mind in building this business. One of the great things about persisting is that when you keep going, it takes your focus off of the answers you get along the way and puts it on who's *next*.

When you get to the point where you no longer need to keep score, you can win this game. The day you stop worrying about answers or reactions as you share this, and just become "a caring sharing machine," is the day you start to become a successful leader. That's the day when you make the decision to begin building a huge business, no matter *what* challenges you may have to overcome.

The Wheel Has Already Been Invented

You meet someone who seems to be excited about doing something to generate some additional income. You begin to build the dream and share this opportunity. As you do, they'll probably get more excited, become more interested, and get more committed to making it happen. Then you share with them some basics of the system and get them plugged into a leadership-sponsored event where they can learn more. You commit to helping them every step of the way, and you agree to match their efforts. Next, you set aside another couple of evenings so they can bring in a few friends and you can repeat the process. You promote the system to everyone who gets in your business.

What I've just done is repeated to you what has been repeated to me and millions of others in this business through the years. It's been repeated for only one reason. It works! It even worked before there was support material and any tools to speak of. It worked better when people began reading books and listening to tapes. It worked when videos came into use. And now it's working even better with the power of the Internet.

Now that you know that, why on earth would you want to spend one single second trying to come up with "a better way"? You can duplicate what one leader told me when I first got started. "Go out and achieve success doing it this way and then, if you still want to, you can spend your time finding ways to do it better." Another way of looking at it is to do it their way until you can prove them wrong. You'll find you can't. The system has worked well for years, and it's only getting better.

Say you enjoy fishing. What if someone shares the secret location of their favorite fishing hole, shows you pictures of the record setting fish they caught there, and then gives you their rod and the lures they used to catch those fish? Would you get to the location and look for another spot? Would you use another rod, lures and different bait? Not if you really wanted to catch fish.

When someone successful is willing to give you all the tips and information it took for them to achieve their success, why would you want to "reinvent the wheel"? Listening to sound advice and applying it actually makes you a "trailblazer" in your own life so you can change your situation or lifestyle. Be among the people who say they're going to be "trailblazers" and then do whatever it takes to succeed.

With this business, you have the opportunity to create success and wealth in your life by doing something average-thinking people won't do. And the best part is, you don't have to figure it out for yourself what to do. The system is already proven and in place. And now you have the power of the Internet that could multiply your results, and therefore expedite your reaching your goals and dreams. Its presence in the business can have a positive influence on your sponsoring more independent business owners. And this means that more products and services can be used by each one because of the huge "mall" on the Internet that they can take advantage of. In addition to that, you'll also have people "coming on board" as retail customer clients, as well as discount buying members. And who knows? After a while, some of these folks might also want to become independent business owners as the benefits of the opportunity dawns on them.

A Solid System And Duplication Makes Your Life Simpler And Easier

In addition to writing books, I travel around the country as a professional speaker and trainer. While it's always wonderful to speak to the fired up people in the business, I also speak to corporate America. The challenge with that is, the corporate people all have different needs and want different programs. I need to sit with them every time, prior to speaking, to design a program that's specific for their company's situation.

With the duplication business, you'll never have to worry what you're teaching to one person as opposed to another. You teach them all basically the same thing, perhaps with a different emphasis, depending on their needs. The other benefit is, when the leaders are at a function speaking to your people at a seminar or other event, they teach the same thing they've taught you to do and teach.

As your business grows, and you're helping your people, it's so much easier to be able to pick up where someone left off and continue with what they started. This continuity adds to the credibility of the business, your leadership, your people, and to you. You're all "on the same sheet of music." It's also much easier to teach something that's being taught all around you. The person learning can absorb it faster. They hear about the system from all the leaders, which reinforces what you're teaching them. And as they observe others successfully following the system, this helps them feel confident that it's the right thing to do and it works.

How Powerful Can The System Be?

Suppose you're so busy that you're only squeezing in, for example, a couple of hours a week for the business. But rather than be discouraged, you have a dream and you decide to use those hours to your best advantage. Using the system and the tools from your leadership, you find that if you work at it, you can sponsor one person each month. Say that person you sponsored the first month has the necessary dreams, desires, and drive, but they have only a couple of hours a week as well. They also discover that they can sponsor one person each month by doing this. What could this lead to?

First of all, the good news is, you've doubled the size of your business! But what if that was all you'd be able to do for the whole first year? Well, assuming that all the people you sponsored were only able to do what you did, I think you'll be surprised at the potential results. Let's see...

As I said, the first month you sponsored one person. Now there are two people in your business. The second month you sponsor someone and then there are three, right? Nope. The first person you sponsored also sponsored someone that month. Remember, in this example, everyone you sponsor duplicates only what you do. In real life some may sponsor more, and some less. We're dealing with people here — not robots!

In the third month you'd go from four to eight. Fourth month 16, and so on. At the end of the year you could have as many as 4,096 people, in your business, *if* everyone sponsors one person a month! Now suppose we follow the 95 percent rule. This means that 95 percent of this will not happen. Most people will just continue to do what they were doing to "get by."

You'd still have over 200 people in your business. Which in theory, if you carried it out another year, the math says you'd have hundreds of thousands in your business! Realistic? No. Math is an exact science and cannot be argued with. The human element, however, introduces that unpredictable quality we talked about earlier. Consider dealing with people as a great, fun adventure.

Now suppose you only had those 200. (Keep in mind, in this fictional scenario, you only had to actually personally sponsor 12 people to do this.) All they did was spend an average of $100 to $500 a month on products and services available on the Net — products and services they're already using anyway. In that case, you'd have a business that is generating between $240,000 and $1,200,000 volume a year. If you earned 5 percent of that, not counting bonuses and other incentives, you'd receive between $12,000 and $60,000 extra a year. I'd say that's "PG" (pretty good), how about you?

And all that could happen just after a year's work, but it could also take longer. However, now with the power available through the use of the Internet, people can do it larger and faster. It's totally up to you how much effort you put in. It's your business and you're your own boss. Your best bet is to follow the system and do what's been working for others who've already succeeded, perhaps even before the Internet came into the picture. Just imagine what *you* can do with your business — now that you have e-commerce to enhance your efforts! If you'll commit to following the system and really applying yourself to the business for just a year, you're likely to be very glad you did. And what if you devote perhaps five to ten hours or more each week to your business activities?

Why Do Some People Give Up?

Your perception is your reality. Ever hear that expression? What it means is that no matter what you say about a situation, the way people see it in their own minds will determine the truth for them. You need to do your best to help people create an accurate perception. Consider the following scenario...

Let's say you meet a nice young couple in the line at your neighborhood grocery store. After chatting for a while you realize they definitely have the spark you look for when approaching someone about your business. You start building a little friendship in the store and then talk some more in the parking lot, before unloading your groceries into your car. As the conversation proceeds, they actually confess that they have been looking for something they could do together, since it seems they're always apart, working two jobs. A week later you give them a call, recalling your chance meeting. You ask if they were serious about what they said. They say "yes," and you set up an appointment to share the business with them.

Since your wife doesn't work outside the home, you decide to impress these young folks while making them feel relaxed. In consideration of the fact that they'll be coming over right after work, your wife prepares a nice dinner for them, using your best china and crystal. When they arrive, the entire house smells wonderful.

You sit down to a lovely meal, enjoy their company, and get to know them a bit more. Perhaps you even begin setting the tone for sharing more about the business by discussing their dreams over dessert. Now it's time for the actual plan. As you go through it, perhaps sharing a video or a CD-Rom and showing them the website, or whatever you've been taught to do, all the signs begin pointing in the right direction. There's a lot of head nodding and excitement. Everything seems to be going beautifully.

You close the evening by setting up a time to get back with them to help them get started. In the meantime you give them some information (some literature and perhaps a book, an audiotape, a video tape, or a CD-Rom) to look over before your next get together. As they drive away, you know you've got a great couple that you'll love working with to help them build this business.

On the scheduled follow-up day you show up, and much to your surprise, they decline. You can't understand what happened. The reality for you was, you had an awesome dream session. The plan went incredibly well, and they asked all the right questions. Even as they were leaving you could hear the excitement in their voices. Your perception of reality said you did it all right.

But what about *their* perception? This is what they could have said to each other in their car on the way home:

Husband: "Wow! They are wonderful people, so friendly and nice. Won't it be great working with them? And the idea of using the Internet sure sounds good to me."

Wife: "It really looks like a super opportunity and they seem like the right people for us to work with. But there is *one thing* I'm worried about."

Husband: "What is it?"

Wife: "They show this to people four or more times a week and we both work. Who do you think will be cooking all those meals?"

Husband: "That's something I hadn't thought of. Plus, the cost of all that extra food and china and crystal — we don't have nice tableware like they do either."

Wife: "Maybe this just isn't a good time."

Husband: "Too bad. I really thought this could be our chance. If you don't want to do it honey, I understand."

Learn How To Express Not Impress

I know in my heart that it would not have been your intent to create that impression. Unfortunately, when you offer people an opportunity to change their lives, most of them are bound to look at all the potential challenges before diving headlong into anything. That's called healthy skepticism. The impression you created became a reality for them. They made their decision based on what *their* eyes saw and their interpretation of that — not necessarily what you intended for them to see.

Be careful. Only do what the system recommends — things that can be duplicated by anyone, and that encourage people to want to be in (and stay in) the business with you. In the previous example, do you think their excitement level would have been any less had you just served coffee in styrofoam cups, with some light snacks on paper plates (all bought from your business)? Of course not.

While serving coffee and snacks without fancy tableware certainly wouldn't have guaranteed that this couple would have gotten in the business, it would have eliminated some objections that could have been avoided in the first place. Remember, it's much more important to *express* yourself and do what is duplicatable, rather than trying to impress others with how good you are or what you have.

You Can't Fix What You Can't See

People who successfully build this business typically achieve their goals by helping others achieve theirs. They need to support their people to work through whatever challenges may arise. Some may need help prospecting. Others may need assistance with the start-up of a new prospect. Still others may need to develop their people skills so they can retain the people they sponsor. And some will need help with the Internet. Fortunately, the system offers lots of tools like books, tapes, seminars, other tools and mentoring which can help you tremendously.

When everyone uses the same system of duplication, it's much simpler to identify and resolve a challenge. It can often be easily isolated and, with some guidance, perhaps from your leader, corrected.

However, if everyone were doing things as they independently chose to do them, it would be virtually impossible to correct or guide anyone. How could you recommend changes if you can't even figure out what they're doing in the first place? And if that's the case, how can you observe that something is being done incorrectly if you have no standard to go by? Without a system that is easy to duplicate, this business wouldn't have grown like it has. Its proven success and simplicity has enabled people to keep on keeping on so they can reach their goals.

Such a successful proven system gives people the confidence that they too can succeed. They simply need to duplicate what already works. Without a system, many would think like 95 percent of the population who are "comfortable" in their existence (rut). They say only the "lucky few" make it and it could never happen for average people like themselves — which just isn't true.

Following the system, duplicating the successful efforts of others, and honestly caring about your people are key to building a solid foundation and growing your business. It all works together. And when you can't quite figure out what to do next, either the system or your mentor has the answers, or can get them.

Imagine how difficult your life would have been if you would have had to figure everything out for yourself. For you former Little Leaguers out there, what kind of a baseball player would you have been if there had been no one around for you to copy? Didn't that make it easier for you to first see yourself hitting the ball, and then actually doing it?

Remember high school chemistry. What do you suppose would have happened if you didn't copy and duplicate the teacher's instructions exactly? You may have created destruction rather than a constructive formula!

Duplicating is a natural part of life. It's not something new. Now you have the opportunity to maximize the use of this same principle to build your road to your dream. Share and be an excellent example of using the principle of duplication. Couple this with the excitement of using the Internet to show others how they can achieve their dreams with this business. Then they can go out and do the same thing with others…and it continues…!

"Already 28% of America's population has a business in the home — that's nearly 34 million home based businesses... this will grow at least 50% within this decade."

Success Magazine

Chapter Ten

What Will They Need You For?

"No one can succeed without the cooperation of other, like-minded people. The power of the Internet helps you attract more people into what is now a 'high-touch, high-tech' business."

They Did Okay Before You Came On Board

When you understand the principles that make a company successful, you can better comprehend why it does what it does. When a corporation is doing several billion dollars a year and they want to grow to the next level, they need to *add to* their formula of success. They just don't scrap what got them to where they are and start over. They build on their already strong foundation.

This business was founded on and has flourished by providing anyone, who wants a chance to succeed, the opportunity to do so. Regardless of their background, people can achieve whatever they're willing to work for and be given the necessary support to do so. This has always been true for this business. And it is even more so now that the Internet is a key part of it. It can play a central role in everyone's ability to far surpass their previous accomplishments.

Since the very beginning, this business has been built on the fact that your success is based on your willingness to devote your time to helping others achieve their success. *It's a people business, pure and simple, first and foremost. And the addition of the Internet doesn't change that philosophy one iota!* Quite the contrary. Using the Internet makes it more important than ever! The business could have continued doing billions each year, as it was. But, the founders and leaders chose to continue their tradition of constant improvement. They are always working to make all aspects of this business better for the people growing their businesses and for the customers/clients and members they serve.

Case in point. What if they had sworn all their current independent business owners to secrecy and said that the Internet was only for those who were already in the business? Then, where would the growth come from, besides, of course, potential increases in existing independent business owner and customer/client consumption? Instead, they thought of everyone. Here is an exciting new opportunity to grow yourself, and your business, whether you've been in the business for awhile, or are brand new.

If you're reading this book and have never seen anything like this before, congratulations! You're one of the reasons all this has been developed. You might never have been interested in seriously going for your dreams until you saw that cutting edge 21st century technology is being used. Now you can better understand why your prospects, now and in the future, need you. No one else may ever think of them otherwise. They may appear satisfied with their standard of living and their homes and cars. But they could be deeply in debt — even on the verge of bankruptcy — and desperate for someone to notice and possibly help them. People's appearances can be "foolers." The ones who really "look good" could be in the most trouble of all. To look that good often means they're broke at a higher lifestyle — owing "everybody and his uncle."

When someone who's experienced in this business observes all of the advances that are being made to better help people build their futures, their confidence and belief, although it may have been strong before, just has to be soaring. What other company would risk millions of dollars and untold people-hours just so you can go out and share their opportunity with more people to build *your* business? Support like this in any other industry is virtually unheard of.

Technology Magnifies Success

If you're just looking at the business or a brand new independent business owner starting out, you now have the best chance at success this opportunity has ever offered. If you're already in the business, whatever results you have been getting in the past, by using the Internet, you now have the potential to magnify them many times over. That's great news. If you have been plugging away, building your business gradually and keeping going because you had faith in the system, this high-tech tool opens new doors of opportunity. You can build even bigger on your previous efforts. Even if you have just been enjoying the fine array of products and services, getting inspired by staying plugged into the system, and have some customers — but haven't been building the business — that's fine too. You may want to take advantage of this Internet opportunity and launch your business now, with all the excitement that's been generated. You probably know a number of people who would be enthusiastic about joining you in your new enterprise!

The time to plan how you'll build your business is right now. Get excited about your dream and everything you can do to be successful with this business. Request a schedule of events from your leadership and prioritize your schedule so you can attend them. Ask about what tools, like videos and audiotapes, books, literature, perhaps a CD-Rom, are available to help you. Ask your leader to help you to map out a plan of action. Tell others about the system and encourage them to use it. You may be able to do that with quite a few people right away — as you get the word out about what's happening with the power of the Internet.

Consistently invest the time and effort to share what this business can do for people and how they can use the system to grow. As you continue to grow, it can pay big dividends. This also helps you keep your business on the fast track, as people duplicate you. Without your guidance and that of those who are helping you, your people would be left to figure it out for themselves — and that just doesn't produce results. You need to keep reinforcing the system of duplication and the need to care about and help others.

Slave Or Master

What determines if something is a tool or a crutch? In the process of building this business the common definitions don't apply. In other arenas, overuse of an item can tend to make it a crutch. But in building this business, using one particular tool that works for you is not that at all. It's just the opposite. With this business, that's what is *supposed* to happen.

However, there is always a small danger that some may think that any tool will accomplish their goals all by itself. The newest tool, the Internet, is viewed perhaps as a revolution, rather than the latest evolution in a series of tools designed to make you more effective in reaching your dreams and goals. Due to the power the Internet brings to bear, this is understandable. However, when that happens, there may be, on some people's part, a tendency to blame it for any results that are less than expected. The Internet will do its part, but it can only enhance your efforts — not replace them.

Whether or not you get the results you want is often determined by control. When you are in control, the tools you use *serve* your needs. Those tools are actually a form of *leverage* you can use to excite people about this business. You could be trying to build a business without them. But your success would take a longer time — if you would be successful at all! Instead, you may choose to use tools so you can attract more people, better demonstrate the power of this business, and teach your people once they're on-board. Most importantly, you can now show others, who may not be as sure of themselves as you are, the great tools that are available to them to help them build their businesses. This along with the system, could give them the reassurance they need.

If the "control" is "delegated" to the tool, a strange thing happens. Nothing! When you take the people element out of a people business, you'll find that, in most cases, people aren't interested. People are the heartbeat of the business — it's the relationships that hold the business together. As soon as you rely on any tool to do the work for you, you are, in essence, granting that tool control. That means you may be relying on that tool to create excitement for the prospect all by itself. You may be expecting the technology to generate leads and prospects for you. It can support you in doing that, but it won't do it for you.

Tools *enhance* and carry your message. Using tools *adds* credibility to your opportunity. The Internet is an incredibly powerful tool and undoubtedly can be a strong ally in your building your business. But it, in and of itself, will never have the ability to care about people and inspire them to dream like your interest and encouragement can. As a servant however, this terrific technology can help people envision even better how their future could be different by building this business.   But, just by itself, the Internet can't give people their dream. A dream is something very special that comes from deep inside each of us. And, it usually takes someone who cares about us to help us coax it out.

Tools, whether they're new technology or table saws, are incapable of creating anything if they are the masters. If you stand back and look at a piece of wood near a saw, how long do you believe you'll have to watch it before the saw takes action, and cuts that wood to size? As long as you let the tool stay in control, the results are easy to predict. Look at what the tool did without you yesterday and the exact same thing will happen today, unless and until you "team up" with it as its master to make it happen.

Once you become the master of your tools, you become the master of your future. Only you can share your enthusiasm to help your people get excited enough to decide to even read, look at, or listen to your tools. Only you can get others to share their dreams and, with your tools, show them there is more hope than ever that those dreams can really come true.   Only *you* can help others discover the tremendous power and potential of this e-commerce business. And only *you* can show them the support — in the form of tools, concern, and leadership, which is available to them, regardless of their current situation. A tool can't listen, give someone a hug, an encouraging pat on the back, or a smile. But *you* can, and you will, if you really want to grow.

It's Only A Decision Away

When asked what they'd like to accomplish in life, most people would answer that they'd like to "be successful." However, later in life most of those same people would admit that success has eluded them. With some rare exceptions, many had everything they needed to succeed — yet somehow still got stuck in mediocrity. What happened?

In many cases, they continued the tradition of "fitting in," "following the crowd," and "just getting by." This is yet another way of saying *getting used to not getting what you could out of life.* Even though they could look and marvel at others who have "made it," they somehow never quite believed it was possible for them to do it too. And even if they did believe, to whatever degree, that they could excel, most never got around to asking a successful person for help or guidance. In many cases, they may not have even considered the idea.

After a while, they may have simply given up on their dreams. And even when someone offered to share with them ways to change their life, there would be a sigh, a weak smile, and of course the phrase, "Hey, I'm doing okay. I can pay the bills."

The key ingredient missing here is what's missing for most people — the *quality decision* to do something to change their life. Until you or someone you're working with decides to make a change in their life, the marvelous Internet and all the amazing potential it represents, will fall on deaf ears. A *person*, a real live human being, as old fashioned as it may sound, needs to intervene and help the other person get out of their own way. They need to give them hope — that it's *never* too late to strive for their dreams. Until a breakthrough in thinking can be accomplished, such a decision simply won't be made. Their old thinking will lead them down their old, worn out path. However, once a person makes a solid decision to use whatever tools they need to use, and does whatever it takes to achieve their goals and dreams, things will start happening. Their thinking then becomes to their advantage!

Without commitment though, everything else is just information and conversation. The fact that you're in this business, or seriously considering it, is a great first step. When you've made the decision to take action and commit to it, then you can *really make strides* in the direction of your dreams and goals.

Just keep in mind what Robert Louis Stevenson once said:

"Whatever we are, it is but a stage on the way to somewhere else, and whatever we do, however well we do it, it is only a preparation to do something else that shall be different."

Keep going toward your dreams, regardless of the outcomes along the way. The Internet is a powerful tool and can help you accomplish great things when it's in the hands of a person with a dream.

"The Greatest Opportunity On Planet Earth"

Based on decades of results, it has been proven over and over again that this business is a resounding success. It brings a message of hope that anyone with a dream, regardless of age, sex, nationality, knowledge, education, background, or experience, can create a better life for themselves and those they care about.

The message is very clear. The great system that has been in place since early on will continue showing there is hope for those who want more out of life. The strong leadership continues to work with and help create more new leaders every year. But the message of hope needs to be delivered, to reach even more "hungry" people.

No matter how great the message is though, its impact can only be felt after the messenger completes their delivery. Even the greatest of messages has no power to help anyone if it is kept a secret. Its power increases only as more people are told of its importance. And that's where you come in.

By your willingness to share this message of hope with others, you can increase your own chances for success — as long as you take the necessary action. Your ability to help others, or to show them where they can get the help they need, can grow with practice. Your compassion and wisdom will increase along the way and will create more strength in you and in your ability to nuture your growing business. You, everyone who came before you, and those who will come after you, are the messengers that help make this "The Greatest Opportunity on Planet Earth."

The Timing Is Perfect

You may have been at this business for a while and are always using the tools that make it better. You may also be brand new, or perhaps you're still in the process of taking a look at the business. Everyone is in a little different stage of the game.

Since this is a business, you need to provide the best possible products and services at fair prices. The Internet will enable you to offer an enormous line of products at competitive prices which will be delivered with a speed unheard of just a few years ago. Those of you who have been working at this for a while can now offer an even bigger opportunity, with a whole new expanded dimension of products and services, to the people who may not have been interested before. The Internet just seems to attract people like a magnet.

If you are considering whether this might be a worthwhile opportunity for you, you may need to take a look at where things are heading.   You want to be associated with a business that's on the cutting edge that has enormous potential. Right? You probably want to be ready to "ride the crest of the wave" of positive potential as it surges in the new millenium. Correct? Current surveys show that only about 10 percent of the population is using the Internet for purchases. Within two to five years, though, the predictions are that 90 percent will be on-line shoppers. That's nothing less than an opportunity for amazing growth!

That gives you two to five years and millions of people to share this with. If there is something out there with more potential for any individual or couple to create a lifelong stream of income, I haven't seen it. If you know of anything, tell me what it is.

Potential alone has never made anyone well off. Taking dedicated action however, even years back when there was certainly less potential, has created financial freedom for those who made the effort and did it anyway. A human being or a company needs to be constantly experiencing growth, or stagnation sets in. And the people in this business, along with the corporate supplier, have been growing for years. Remember, there is *no* status quo. We either improve or we get worse. Time marches on. Are you marching with it?

Of Dreams And Machines

You and people like you are the most important and necessary ingredient to the success of this business. But more importantly, you are the most significant and necessary ingredient of your *own* success. While the Internet is rapidly changing how this business is done, you need to explore and discover the "WHYs" that make people want to do this, or anything else, for that matter.

Without your interest, encouragement, and help there is a possibility that some people may end up sitting in front of computer screens waiting for their business to just happen! They simply may not understand what a key role they play in their business — even though they now have the power of the Internet at their disposal. They may not know quite what to do next. If that should occur, it probably wouldn't take very long for them to lose sight of their dreams and goals, and eventually give up.

So, you need to guide them in the right direction. If you know very little about computers, no problem! It is a tool that anyone can learn to use. Someone can teach you how to use the Internet. Maybe even a friend who's well-versed on the Web can help you, while you share how this business could give them their future! People need inspiration and guidance. Information alone will not make anyone successful. They need to know you care about them and to see the enthusiasm you have for this business — and the potential it has to support *them* in achieving *their* dream. You need to help them see what tremendous strides they can now make, toward realizing their dream, as long as they are committed to their future and take the necessary action. Benjamin Franklin put it well when he said, "Perform without fail what you resolve."

"If you feel tied down now, doing what you're currently doing, this business as a vehicle — enhanced by the Internet and e-commerce — can help you set yourself free."

Chapter Eleven

The More Things Change, The More They Stay The Same

"The work of the individual still remains the spark that moves mankind ahead."
Igor Sikorsky – Inventor of the Helicopter

Tech Realities

Do you have any credit card bills? If you do, get the most recent one and take a look at some of the things you bought last month. Many of those items probably weren't even available a decade ago. Things are changing faster today than ever before.

Part of the reason for this rapid change is the constant improvement in the ways we exchange information. Years ago, if you were looking to share an idea, it may have taken *weeks* for a letter to travel across the country. Soon, it could be done by telegraph, which was faster, but you often had to travel a distance with your horse and buggy to the telegraph office.

As mentioned previously, the telephone came along and changed communications.   You could speak to people anywhere instantly, right from your own home.   The only drawback was you probably had to wait if you wanted to leave a message for someone in a different time zone, or who wasn't home or in their office at the time. Voice mail and answering machines had not yet been invented!

As we begin the new millenium, the Internet is dramatically changing the way we communicate. It's given us another option. While an idea is still fresh in your mind, you can instantly send it virtually anywhere in the world. You can even send it to thousands of people at the same time. Some corporations are even letting people set up offices in their homes and having them tele-commute. They can now work their jobs from home, where they are most comfortable. It doesn't matter where their computer is — in an office building, in their home office, or on their lap in an airplane. They can do their job anywhere. And if they get up at 4 a.m. they may be able to begin their workday and be finished at 2 in the afternoon.

The one ingredient that is threaded throughout our history and all the wonderful advancements that were made is the individual who, in spite of any and all obstacles, persistently *kept on going*. These people focused totally on the outcomes they were striving for — the benefits others could reap from their inventive ideas. They regarded the setbacks along the way only as minor incidents, as compared to the great dream they were pursuing. Today, new discoveries can happen even more quickly because of advancing technology. But it isn't high-tech equipment that makes these dreams a reality. It's still those individuals with a big dream, a strong desire, and the commitment to see it through, who make the biggest differences in our lives.

Building Your Business Is Child's Play

It was September 1996. We were approaching my daughter Katie's sixth birthday. I was leisurely having a cup of coffee at the breakfast bar, when she climbed up onto the stool next to me. "Daddy, I know what I want for my birthday." I thought that since I was going away on speaking engagements for the next few weeks, that this information would certainly be helpful, and it would save me a lot of time and trouble. "That's great Katie. What is it?"

I smiled at her. I had purposely asked her an open-ended question, without any guidelines for an answer. She replied excitedly, "I want a guinea pig." This caught me by surprise, and I almost choked on my coffee as I tried not to show my reaction!

The challenge with having any more pets was, we already had an overweight and slobbering Black Lab who thinks *he's* the center of attention. And my son John had a four-and-a-half-foot-long Florida King Snake, living with him in his bedroom! So, I looked at her and said the first thing that popped into my mind. "Daddy doesn't know too much about guinea pigs. I'll have to check it out and get back to you."

Later that day, I had arrived at the location of my first speaking engagement a bit early and took some time out and located a pet shop in a nearby mall. I walked in and asked them to tell me all about guinea pigs. I figured anything I could use as ammunition not to get one would be very helpful. All they could tell me, though, was that you should never keep a guinea pig in an enclosed glass cage! Not being very familiar with this type of animal, I asked, "Why not?"

Of course the person answering me is the one wearing the "TRAINEE" badge! He says, "We have one over here and

I'll show you." This pet store had glassed-in viewing areas where we found a guinea pig that had been in there for about an hour. When the trainee opened the door, my eyes began tearing up. It smelled like someone had sprayed the room with "Barnyard in a Can"!

No way was any guinea pig getting into *my* house. But wait. It was my daughter's birthday wish. I didn't want to disappoint her or have her be angry with me. I had to think about this one....

Then it dawned on me. She's only going to be six. I'm supposed to be a professional speaker and sales training expert. I'll convince her that she doesn't even *want* this thing. I couldn't wait to get back home and show her who's the master of this situation.

One of the things I really focus on when I'm speaking is to let the audience know that they need to get very specific with what they want and focus on it as if they have already achieved it. I figured that any principle that's of value to my audiences, would also be of value to my family.

As I walked into the house, Katie greeted me with a larger than usual hug and said, "Daddy, I know *exactly* what kind of guinea pig I want. Tan with a 'bad hair day.'" Gulp.

I sat down with Katie and began to lay out my nuggets of negativity. "Katie, this is a big responsibility. Who's going to feed this animal?" There was no delay in the response. "You get the guinea pig nuggets and you put them in a bowl and it can eat anytime it wants to." Well, I lost that one but I thought *for sure* I'd have her with this one. "Who's going to clean the cage?" She surprised me with her answer. "Mommy." I gave her that one!

As the days passed, I continued sharing my barrage of potential problems. Sometimes it's hard to see if you're getting through to a child. I was determined and pressed on.

Finally, it's the Saturday before her birthday and, as only kids will do, she burst into our bedroom early in the morning.

"Daddy, I thought about all you said." I looked at her with my understanding look while inside I was doing a victory roll. "Yes," I replied trying to hide my relief. "Daddy, if that guinea pig ever gives us any problems, we'll just feed it to Johnny's snake!"

As I wrote my books over the next couple of years, I heard that little rodent running on that wheel in her cage. When I started to get frustrated with my inability to concentrate, I remembered the lesson I had learned and felt grateful instead.

Are You Acting Like An Adult?

Throughout the previous story, I used all my life experiences and ingenuity to come up with ways not to have another pet in our home. I reasoned with logic. I searched and found every potential problem that could arise as a result of keeping that animal in our house. But these problems I relayed fell on deaf ears.

My daughter was focused on the prize. She was convinced that no matter what the problems may be, it would be worth it. She could handle the love and care (through delegation!) needed by "her" guinea pig. I was focused on all the negative aspects. I had tried to steal her dream. I never looked for any solutions — I only looked for problems. Katie kept her eye on her little dream, and never considered the problems — only the solutions! She knew that once that guinea pig was hers, any problems could be handled.

Whenever I'm speaking to a crowd who needs to be motivated, I tell that story. I share how grateful I am for having a guinea pig in my home. I have been taught business-building lessons from leaders and other successful people, but I finally "got it" from a child. Focus on what you want, not the problems or challenges associated with getting it.

Are You Focused Or Finding Excuses?

Before we had access to the exciting new electronic technology of the Internet at our disposal, there were people all around the world in this business. Unfortunately, some of those people chose to focus on the potential challenges they might encounter in building this business—rather than the marvelous possibilities. They allowed their negative thinking to hold them back from achieving their dreams.

Even with all the obstacles people had to overcome (the main one being themselves!), literally thousands grew their businesses to a substantial size. They now have more options and independence than at any other time in their lives. These leaders offered to help anyone who wanted the same opportunity. But many people felt they were the lucky ones — fortunate enough to have gotten in at "the right time."

Today, with the Internet and e-commerce, that's all changed. The right time to build the business *is now*. There can be no excuse. Sure, some people may choose to invest in a computer, if they don't have one. But they don't have to. They can subscribe to a TV web service, like the supplier corporation offers, telephone, an e-mail service, or go to their public library and use one of their computers. There are some folks who may be a bit unsure about this whole thing. That's okay. It's normal to have some reservations about anything new. It's called fear of the unknown, and has been around for a long time. It's perfectly natural and not to be criticized.

In spite of some initial concerns on some people's parts, thousands more will jump on the high-tech bandwagon and achieve the independence they've been wanting — perhaps for years. Still others will do just enough to change their lives, perhaps through a less sizable increase in income and a huge increase in their personal development. Like I mentioned, there will always be those who take this e-commerce opportunity and run with it — who achieve their desired level of success and maybe more.   There will inevitably be some individuals who will think these folks who do whatever it takes and win big, must be either computer experts or at the very least — lucky.

Why is it that some people can achieve success, even without all the advantages of today's technology, while others, with equal ability, can't seem to get started — even with all the advancements on their side? The answer lies with what you focus on.

When you are consistently focused on your destination, and take full advantage of the tools that were developed to help you get there, you're bound to arrive. You need to fix your focus on your dream, plug yourself and your people into the system, develop and rely on your dogged determination to make it happen, ask for help as necessary, and simply use the many carefully-designed tools as needed. If you dwell on the possible challenges you may encounter as you use the tools, the Internet, or anything else, you'll be sabotaging your own desired success. Besides, most of the things we worry about never happen anyway. (Thank goodness!)

What you focus on magnifies. Concentrate on your dreams and goals and your heartfelt desire to achieve them, and you'll continue to grow. Conversely, if you dwell on setbacks, large or small, your focus causes them to overshadow your dreams, leading to a diminishing of your desire to achieve. It's a downward spiral — you don't want to go there! The bottom line is, you get what you focus on. Focusing on achieving your dreams and goals could mean you'll have a whole new exciting lifestyle. Whereas, finding fault with every little incident creates a habit of putting things off — because of perceived potential challenges and imperfections. So it just makes sense to focus on what you want — rather than any challenges! You can deal with the "imperfections" as you go along.

To clear the air once and for all, nothing's perfect. The human element guarantees this. Every business has imperfections. Those who are serious about their desires and dreams overlook or work around what they may perceive to be "wrong." They use what has definitely worked in the past to help them achieve. They realize that no tool can do everything. In the case of the Internet, it can tremendously enhance your efforts to propel yourself to the next level and beyond. The rest is up to you.

Looking for problems is a dangerous habit. Look for difficulties and they'll surely pop up. Use them as a reason to stay where you are in life and you'll do just that. Dwell on them and you may find that things could even get worse. *Focus on what you want* — not what you don't want.

What has always thrilled me is that we all have a choice about the direction we take in life. You can choose what you focus on in life just as easily as choosing what you'll eat for dinner. Choose to focus on problems and your life will probably be filled with them. Case in point — some people continue for years, living paycheck-to-paycheck, and say they could have done better if it weren't for all those problems. What they may not realize is that everyone has their share of challenges — whether it looks like it or not. Your best bet is to choose to focus on solutions, and your life will be filled with them! Sound like a good deal?

Decide on your destination and you'll find that many of your problems disappear. For example, it's *so much easier* to put up with a job you don't particularly like when you are working on your financial freedom and know that it's only temporary. Having limited free time right now, while you build your business, doesn't seem so bad when you realize that your efforts will be rewarded down the road — when you'll be able to come and go as you please.

The nice thing is, the Internet is here to make your dreams and goals even *more* achievable. It offers more solutions, such as management services, to fulfill your business needs. Sure, there may be some challenges along the way. But, so what! Instead, look at the good, for example, how it will help you get in touch with more people with considerably less effort than before. Focus on the fact that it can open the door for you to share your opportunity with a whole new group of people — some of whom wouldn't listen to you before. Focus on the positives and encourage others to do the same.

That reminds me of the story of the shoe company looking to expand its market. As I recall, the company president sent a veteran salesperson to a South Pacific island to drum up some new business. When the salesperson got there, he looked around and observed that no one was wearing any shoes. The next day, he called the president and said, "I'm coming home. Nobody here wears shoes."

Before he got back, the president called in his newest salesman, who had just recently graduated from college. He told him he wanted him to take a trip to that same island to see what kind of business he could find. When the young man arrived, he noticed no one was wearing any shoes. Excited, he rushed to a phone and called the president. He said to him, almost out of breath, "Sir, get those sandal-making machines cranking. Everybody here is barefoot!"

The veteran salesman only saw a problem, while the young man saw a solution — a golden opportunity. Destinations and roadblocks are the realities of those who think of them. If you allow yourself to focus on the perceived difficulties and let the fear of them grow inside you, you magnify them and they become *real problems*. When you keep your destination firmly pictured in your mind as real and attainable, you'll do everything you need to do to bring you closer to achieving it — until you actually do. Simply put, it all depends on your point of view. And the great news is...*you* get to pick the view!

"When you see the possibilities for yourself, you'll see the opportunity."

Chapter Twelve

Welcome To
The 21st Century!

*"Those who succeed in life always embrace change.
He who hesitates is lost."*

They Will See It When They Believe It

Beginning the 21st century means different things to different people. People everywhere are excited about the great possibilities that are coming. They believe this is the dawn of a new beginning — a chance to make a difference in their lives and in the lives of those they care about. These people can see themselves growing and developing — getting better at what they do and who they are.

The turn of a century is a major event. The dawn of a new millenium is an incredible time to be alive. But so is the birth of a child. I'm certain there are other events in your life that have happened and more will come that could bring about similar excitement or fears. All of these things represent change.

People react differently toward change. Some embrace it as a new possibility. Maybe it's a second chance. Whereas others absolutely detest it. They want *nothing* to do with it. Both types of people react before the predicted change actually occurs, and, amazingly, the way they feel is exactly opposite. Why? Because their beliefs are opposite. What you perceive and then believe becomes your reality.

Positive or negative, your attitude largely determines the reality of your future. When you embrace the new e-commerce approach as a welcomed opportunity, or as a second chance to build a business that will take care of you and your family for life, that's truly what it can be for you.

The 21ˢᵗ century and the Internet offer virtually unlimited horizons. You will either expand them or be stifled. What you believe about the future will become what you experience. What you look for is what you'll find.

The new millenium, with all its potential, is upon us. Whether you choose to participate or watch won't change that. It's happening, regardless. However, what you achieve as a result is totally up to you. You can choose to be a bystander and just watch good things pass you by. Or you can get into it and be an active part of creating a bright, positive future for yourself. Seize the opportunity to decide how many good things will come your way.

As we've said in different ways throughout this book, the choice is totally yours. You decide what happens in your life largely by the choices you make. Not making these choices doesn't excuse you from your responsibility. Deciding not to go with the times, for whatever reason, is a choice, as well. Choose to win — focus on your dreams and goals, persevere, and watch what happens!

Remember, the ever-changing calendar and advancements in technology, in and of themselves, don't change anything.

The calendar simply records the passage of time, while the development of new technology provides us with new products, services, and tools. It's what you do with all those things that will determine what occurs in your future!

It's Not Enough To Just See And Hear

As you finish sharing this fine opportunity with someone you've recently met, you may get the feeling that somehow they didn't get it. They saw the numbers you drew out. They heard about the potential and actual successes people are already having. But somehow, as great as the opportunity is that you shared with them, it just didn't seem to reach them.

Was there something you forgot? Maybe. Did you make it sound too good to be true? Possibly. But before you get too hard on yourself, consider this more common possibility:

Perhaps they truly *did hear* everything you said. Assume you got all the facts straight, the numbers added up, and the support materials backed up everything you said as totally true and credible. Amazing as it may seem, it's still possible they'll choose to do nothing, and walk away. "So, *why* didn't they get it?" you might be asking. "Is there anything I could have done to have made them better understand?"

When it comes to the future of someone's life, they choose what it is they want to understand. If someone is merely "sounding off," complaining about a situation or challenge in their life, rather than sincerely looking to take the necessary actions to improve it — no opportunity, regardless of how great it is or how it's presented, will change their minds. They're generally just looking for sympathy or somebody to commiserate with, rather than someone to give them hope and a way out. I know this boggles the minds of those of us who are positive-thinking and solution-oriented. But it's the truth.

All you can do is do your best to plant the seed of hope. *They* need to water it! You can always leave them the option of changing their mind, and coming to you at some point down the road. You can do that with your compassionate, flexible attitude. Remain upbeat and committed to your goals and dreams. Show them that, while you're certainly willing to help them achieve their goals, their decision not to pursue their own desires, in no way will keep *you* from achieving *yours*. You're simply not hanging your financial future on *their* answer.

In fact, you can even use their "no" as motivation to build a solid business. They may change their mind when they see you moving ahead. Success is the best "revenge"! Use that fact to push yourself to continue growing, and you may actually attract them later to take another look.

Some people need to see an opportunity like this a few times before they truly understand its potential. Often, in the mean time, they get knocked around a bit more in their jobs or "downsized" from their so-called secure careers. This could humble them some and make them more open to change. Regardless of which direction they seem to be going, when you truly care about people, you'll still give them as much of your time as they need to satisfy their concerns. And no matter what they may finally say, you need to maintain the attitude that your door is *always* open. You treat them with the same kindness and consideration that you would want others to have with you.

Getting Them To Say, "How Do You Do That?"

Do you think the use of the Internet's technology will have people lined up at your house, waiting to sign up and build the business? Who knows? It *could* happen — especially as the ranks continue to swell and more people learn about it. But nonetheless, don't sit around and wait for the crowds to start gathering outside your door!

For people to associate with you in business, they generally need to know who you are, where you are, and what you're doing. However, they may not sit still long enough to hear all that information! You need to encourage them to ask you questions.

One of the most effective ways to get people to ask about what you do is an old technique that will always pass the test of time. It fits right in line with the other principles of this business. Ask about *them* first and show a genuine interest in what they do. When you do this, there are two possible reactions: First, they may tell you all about themselves and their work, and then walk away with no concern for you and what you do. Or, they may ask you to talk about what it is you do — either out of curiosity or a sense of obligation.

If they just want to talk about themselves and run, there's a good chance they wouldn't do very well in a people business — at least initially, before they develop themselves via the system. You don't want to chase them — or anybody, for that matter. Perhaps later you'll get a chance to talk with them again, and this time they may give you a natural opening to share what you're doing. If not, go ahead and build your business first, and let them see that you're moving on. You never know, maybe they'll come to you later, after they see how well you're doing!

The second type of reaction is almost as common and a great opportunity to get good at meeting new people — without sounding like a door-to-door salesperson. Out of politeness they ask what it is that you do. The key is to keep your answer "short and sweet." Put them in a position of curiosity, so they can then ask you questions. When that happens, they're taking an interest in you and your opportunity, even if it is out of courtesy, rather than you pursuing them! That could be a good start.

While there are many ways to describe what you do, there are two simple words that can be more powerful than many others — "work with." When you incorporate them into your initial approach, you'll probably find a lot more interest than if you describe what you do. The reason those words seem to work better is they tell people you have a "partnership" with others. Other words could make it sound as though you simply train a person and then they're on their own. Words like these can scare people away. "I show people how...." I start people up ...." "I set people up in business...."

Each of those might suggest the person will end up totally on their own, risking their future on something they know little or nothing about. Forming a "partnership" let's them know you'll be with them for the duration. This gives them a much better feeling about their opportunity to succeed.

> **Prospect:** "So, what do you do?"
> **You:** "I work with people looking to earn extra income on the Internet."

That's all you generally need to say to spark their interest. If you have someone who might be even a little interested, they'll jump in and take over the conversation. These are just some ideas. Use whatever the leadership in your business wants you to use. As long as the prospect is *asking you* questions, your answers will build interest. Let's continue.

> **Prospect:** "How do you do that?"
> **You:** "I help them establish access to products and services on the Internet."

These short, direct answers are likely to create a lot more curiosity than any long-winded explanation ever could. You can then take total control of the conversation and stop giving them any more information. If there's any interest on their part, they're ready to receive more of the details.

You: "I can't promise you anything but, if you're still serious about learning more, I could possibly meet with you over coffee."

Or

You: "You seem to be interested and I may be able to use some help. I'll tell you what. I'd be happy to schedule a time when we could get together over a cup of coffee to explore the possibilities that may exist for you."

One of the ways to stay memorable is to use what advertising experts use — a tag line. This line, usually at the end, is what interests the prospect to want more information. In the case of building a business, you want to take the pressure off the prospect while also making them aware of the fact that this opportunity is really something special.

Prospect: "Okay. Let's schedule some time."
You: "Okay, fine. I'll put you down in my planner for _____. Would that work for you? Look, if something comes up and you can't make it, please give me a call. And I'll have the courtesy to do the same." (You then exchange business cards, perhaps a CD-Rom, or other contact information.)

There it is. You take the pressure off them from feeling that they have to make a decision. You're giving them a choice. You're letting them know you are going to discuss an opportunity that they may or may *not* qualify for. You're showing them that you're busy but willing to keep an open mind about their possibilities. This "posturizing," i.e., not promising them anything, often causes them to want to get together with you and listen to you about the opportunity. It's just human nature at work. When people don't think they can have something, they often want it even more.

Keep Those Questions Flowing!

Now that they've agreed to meet with you, it's important that you don't become a fountain of information that won't turn off. Don't overwhelm them with details. Your reasons for being in the business are not important to them at this point (and maybe never will be). What *is* important is discovering *their* dream and sharing briefly what this business has to offer them.

Use the power of the question. Open-ended questions work the best — questions that require more than a "yes" or "no" answer. You show you have a genuine interest in what they might be looking for which makes them more inclined to listen to what you have to say. It also allows you to "tailor-fit" what you're saying, i.e., focus your explanation of this opportunity in a way that is most beneficial to the person who matters most — the one right in front of you.

Ask them what they know about the Internet. What do they see as the growth potential for those who use it to market their goods and services? What if they had the opportunity to build a business using the Internet as a tool?

As you talk with your prospect, keep asking open-ended questions and listen — focus on them as you relax and forget about yourself. If they're interested in continuing, they may ask how they can learn more about your opportunity. Again, your leadership can help you with what you're to do next — which will probably be to schedule an appointment to show them the plan where there's a computer so you can show them the main website and those of affiliated companies.

Chapter Thirteen

Everybody's Gone Surfin'— On The Internet

"Anything worth doing is worth doing poorly until you can do it well."

You Can Either Read About Swimming Or You Can Actually Do It!

Everyone seems to be an expert these days. Have you noticed that people seem to have an opinion on just about everything? And just as *they* have opinions, *you* have choices. You can work with some people and build a business, or continue doing what you're doing. While you may allow other people's opinions to sway you one way or another, it always comes down to *you* — and the choices you make.

Let's discuss two types of swimming "experts." The first one thoroughly researched the sport of swimming. They read everything they could get their hands on about every swimmer who ever competed in the sport. They reviewed all the swim meets and memorized all the records set. There wasn't any aspect of the sport they didn't know about.

The second person began swimming at an early age. There were thousands of predawn practices followed by hours practicing in the pool in the evening. They "ate and slept" swimming. When they competed, they put everything they had into each event. In the beginning they lost. Eventually though, they began winning. They even broke some records.

Both of these people would be considered experts in their own right. However, given the choice, which one would you prefer to work with? Would it be the one who spent a lifetime *gathering* information? Or would you choose the one who had put out the effort—even at the risk of failure? Would you tend to pick the one who was out there *creating* information for others to use to fine-tune their skills, or the one just studying it?

The growth of your business is determined by the actions you take, especially in the beginning, when you're laying the foundation. Therefore, you need to be talking to people who are out there doing it. Talking with someone who is just gathering information cannot help you do it. You will be more motivated to do something when you know that the person you're talking with has already done it.

I only mention this as a caution for those of you still considering whether or not this business would be for you. Only you can answer that, but I suggest you gather information from the *real* experts. Speak with people who are actually doing something with the business, rather than those who just have information about it. You'll want to team up with someone who is out there doing it. Also ask if you could attend a seminar and meet other successful people in the business — perhaps who are even from your profession.

What's More Important — What This Business Is, Or What It Does For People?

If you have a family with young children, there are certain things you tend to be concerned about. With college costs rising faster than almost any other expense, and medical and dental costs climbing at almost frightening levels, what would happen if you were unable to provide the necessary income?

If you become sick, injured, or even die, would your family be able to continue living as they had while you were earning a salary? That question can often put a lot of pressure on people, unless they can do something about it before an emergency occurs.

Suppose you could put together a plan that would take care of you in the event you were unable to work? It would pay your salary until you were able to go back to your job. All of your bills would be taken care of and the day-to-day living expenses would be covered as well. Now imagine that this plan is available for only a few dollars a day.

Let's take it a step further. Imagine you could put together a package that would protect your family and the future of all its members for less than the cost of a cup of coffee a day. This program would provide you with a steady source of revenue for living expenses, as well as for the future education of your children.

Now, wouldn't you feel more comfortable with something like that, to protect everything you've worked so hard for? Of course you would. And if you currently don't have this protection in place, it has to be a comfort — just knowing it's available. In fact, that's what you could create with this business.

Yet, if I started the conversation by telling you that I'd like to sit you down and discuss insurance for you and your family, I doubt we'd get far enough into an explanation for you to see all the benefits. It's that way with many things that can better our lives. Most people have an opinion about the label — the name we give something. But few would have that same opinion — once all the benefits were explained and they fully understood them.

You'd probably like to share this business opportunity with some of your friends. Ask some questions, find the ones who are looking to do more, or would just like to have a more convenient way of shopping, while saving time and money. Tell them what it could do for them and their families, then show them the website or give them the information they need to access it on their own. If they are interested, they could become a retail customer/client or a member (for a small fee) able to buy products at a discount. Or they could go one step further and want to see the business opportunity and become an Independent Business Owner.

What's The *REAL* Potential?

Potential is what you can expect to realize when appropriate action is taken. Virtually without the Internet, this industry is currently doing over $100 billion dollars a year. And direct personal shopping on the Internet was just over a billion dollars in the month before Christmas! By combining this business with e-commerce, the potential is awesome.

This business is a proven success. And it continues to grow at an accelerated rate now that a huge number of brand name products can be seen, ordered, and shipped with the click of a button. People can earn residual income, even if they're not personally using the Internet and may not even own a computer. You have a proven concept taking full advantage of the best of both worlds — this rapidly expanding industry and e-commerce — the trend for the new millenium.

But the term potential really comes into play when discussing the most important ingredient — *you*. As I said, this industry will do billions of dollars every year and keep growing — with or without you. But your potential isn't even a consideration unless you make a decision to take advantage of this cutting edge opportunity.

When you decide to do something with this, your potential can come in many forms. You can develop as a person through associating with leaders, listening to motivational tapes, reading positive books. You can also attend seminars, conventions, and other leadership-sponsored activities, designed to help those who are serious about changing their lives for the better.

In addition, you will learn financial "secrets" that will help you better manage the money you are currently earning. Then, when you begin to develop a strong residual based income from your business, *you can make your money work for you* — instead of you just working for it.

And you'll have a tremendous opportunity to be able to make a difference in other people's lives. You may be the first person to come along and show them that they have the ability to change their lives for the better. You could be the one to give them back a precious gift — their dreams. You could then work with them until they achieve their goals. As you continue to do this with enough people, you will be able to make your own goals a reality.

It's okay to do it for the money. Because, before the money comes, you'll have to be ready to receive it anyway. Say you're aiming for financial freedom and the change that it will bring to your life and the lives of those you care about. You'll observe that even greater changes will be occurring in your life as you grow your business. You'll become the type of person who deserves every reward that's about to come your way.

Is there any of the previously mentioned potential that doesn't appeal to you? I wouldn't think so. The only guarantee I can give you about this business is if you walk away. If you choose not to participate in this opportunity and not to build your financial security, the potential I've shared with you will certainly be difficult, if not impossible, to reach through conventional everyday means.

Consider this: Most of you who are reading this were around in 1986. Had you taken a chance and invested just over $2,000 in a little-known company called Microsoft and held on to it for just ten years, you'd now be a millionaire. Of course hindsight is always 20/20. But back in 1986 *some people listened, had foresight, and took action!*

Could this be the next "Microsoft" for you? I can't answer that. I can't promise you that you will become a millionaire in this business. That would be up to you to do. But I can promise you that this is the opportunity with which you can make great strides financially, and becoming a millionaire is a real possibility. If you can dream it, you can do it!

Now let's move on to...

One Final Question...

Chapter 14

Are You Living Your Dream?

"You need to have a dream and work with people to succeed. Couple that with using the Internet and you have a cutting edge opportunity for success."

It's Been There All Along...

Wouldn't it be nice if...? Ever ask yourself that question? Wonderful to ponder, isn't it? It's a great question. However, as you answer, do you ever find yourself interrupting your dreambuilding thoughts with statements like, "Yeah, right. Like that could happen to me"? Or, "Who am I kidding? That's for the privileged few — the lucky ones." Your dreams — they're essential for you to keep going. Yet, you may be fighting the very thing your dreams represent — your possibilities!

People who haven't achieved their dreams often *blame* it on their job or business, a lack of time and money, bills, lack of education, the government, the economy, and almost anything else imaginable. Those are simply beliefs of people taking the stance of a victim. They're negative and self-defeating attitudes. Maybe you've convinced yourself that the dream is gone somehow or that somebody stole it. Well it's not and nobody did. It never left, and no one took it!

Nobody can steal your dream unless you let them. No one has that power over you. Nobody can force you to stay where you are. Nobody except you. And now, with the Internet, your potential to make your dream come true has just been accelerated.

The dream is always there for those who truly seek it. You may have to look a little harder, but it's there. The fact of the matter is, most people let themselves be pushed by circumstances while people who win are drawn by their dreams. But first you need to have a dream before you can make it come true. And, once you find it, you need to hold on to it with all your might.

As you strive for your dream, it will cause you to help others. It also helps you keep a positive attitude just thinking about and anticipating it. It enables you to handle any negative situations more easily. And remember, the key to success is to help enough other people get what they want, and as you do, you'll get what you want.

So where can you look for your dreams? How about behind your complaints of too many hours at work? Or under the disappointments about promotions or raises you didn't get? Or maybe it's buried beneath the pressures of raising a family. No matter what though, *your dream is there for the claiming.* You just need to discover it, believe it, and pursue it—no matter what your circumstances are or what others may say. Remember, anybody who rises above the crowd inevitably gets put down by some people. But their opinion just don't matter. After all, they're not in your shoes, and they probably don't know what you want out of life!

Your dream is still alive. You may have just misplaced it along the way, or locked it up in your heart. You may have tried to stake your claim on the good life, yet, you became so busy *making a living*, you may have forgotten how to *make a life*. Unlock the dream in your heart and let it come out in the sunshine. Clear away the clutter that you may have let get in the way. Focus on it and let it light a fire in you so you passionately want it again.

Let go of any negative thinking about your dream. Instead of telling yourself it wasn't meant to be, *do something* to build your dream — to make it bigger in your mind and heart. Focus on the possibilities instead of the challenges. As Robert Browning once said, "Our aspirations are our possibilities."

What do you aspire to? Whatever it is, that's what's possible for you! What *are* your dreams? Take some time to focus on what *could* be.

Would you like to have the time and money to quit your job or sell your conventional business? What would you do? Travel with your family? Play golf around the world? Go fishing? Flying? Sailing? Skiing? Be a full-time parent? Build your dream home?

As you pursue your dreams, consider the value you could provide others with the exciting new Internet opportunity, the vastly increased line of quality products and services, and your compassion. Could you reach out to others who believe they're stuck in an occupation they hate?

Success *is* within your reach—even if you don't quite believe it yet. You may only need to accept one new idea to be on your way to achieving it. You may only need to make one adjustment to your life to become open to the possibilities that exist for you and your family. You need to accept and welcome *change*—it is necessary in order for you to move on.

By Using The Internet You Can Accelerate Toward Living Your Dream

The introduction of the Internet as a tool for building this business offers you a tremendous opportunity to reach out and take ownership of your dreams. Today, in fact, most new millionaires are the first ones to become so in their families. Contrary to popular belief though, only 1 percent of millionaires inherited their wealth.

If you want different outcomes in your life you need to do different things. If you aren't where you want to be in life, and you keep on doing the same things you've been doing, you probably won't get where you want to be. Most people don't realize this and that's often how dreams get stifled. Like them, you too may have buried them under the so-called "security of sameness."

You may have convinced yourself how fortunate you are to have what you have and that it's wrong for you to want more. You may think that's being greedy. But, think again. Since you'll be helping other people to earn the "more," how could that be greedy? Thoughts like that just bury your dream a little deeper and keep you from going for it and realizing your true potential. It's still there; it just may be buried under a mountain of the negative things others have told you and you may have told yourself! Some people use these negative ideas as excuses not to take action. Could that be true for you?

You undoubtedly have many reasons to be grateful for what you have. Gratitude is essential for happiness. But so is building a bigger dream each time you make a dream come true. It's not letting yourself be locked in by what you've achieved so far. Have you accomplished certain things and now, more or less, you're resting on your laurels? If so, that's certainly a choice you're entitled to make. But along with it comes the death of perhaps some pretty important dreams, and also the opportunity to make a difference in other people's lives. "Same old, same old," is what some people say. How about you? If so, would you like that to change?

Yes, embrace the Internet to help you to accelerate your success as you focus on helping others do the same. And those who don't want to build a business can still benefit by being a retail client (customer) or a discount buying member. Everyone can win.

Security Or Freedom?

Many people resist change for fear of losing their "security." However, the very thing they're attached to, which is probably a job, may be the only thing that's robbing them of their *freedom to be secure*. As long as someone else is signing your paycheck, they have options that control you. They can lay you off or cut your pay while dangling the threat of layoffs in front of you. They may even give you a small raise, then ask you to spend what little free time you may have, to work extra hours at home. What kind of security is that? As someone once said, "Security without freedom is worse than insecurity."

This business gives you an opportunity to create your *own* options. Looking for yourself at this increasingly popular way of doing business, now made even more exciting by the addition of the Internet, may be the key to opening the door of possibilities for you — as it has done for millions of others.

Understand, no one is asking you to quit your job to get your business going. Quite the contrary. In fact, you'll probably be encouraged to become an ideal employee at your job, as you build your business on the side! This will be easier than it may sound since your attitude toward your boss is likely to change when you start seeing "the light at the end of the tunnel."

Your confidence level, as well as your knowledge and skills, can increase dramatically when you really apply yourself to building your business. In fact, you'll become so focused on helping other people grow that your employer will probably be glad you're in the business. Working toward a dream helps build better people! To make it work, people need to care about others. How refreshing.

Now take a moment to let go of so-called "security." Fan the sparks of your dreams and start picturing a life of *freedom*. Freedom to get up when you're fully rested — without an alarm clock. Freedom to spend time with your family — to do what you want. Freedom from debt — to increase your possibilities. Freedom to live where and how you want to — to maximize your happiness. Freedom to donate as much time and money as you want to your church and other causes you believe in. Sounds good. Too good? Well this certainly isn't something for nothing. Since anything worthwhile requires effort, building your own business does too. But the rewards can far outweigh the efforts.

One of the great things about this business is that as it grows, unlike most others, it can actually produce more results and income with no increase in your time and effort. That's because your efforts are *leveraged* in association with the efforts of others. That leveraging is now enhanced with the Internet. Everyone who is serious and committed about using this vehicle to build their financial future, is working towards their own goals by duplicating the *system of success* developed and fine-tuned by their leaders. That *power of duplication* can create freedom for those who dare to work at building their own business rather than just depending on a career that has them tied to a job, or a conventional business that claims most of their time and energy.

Freedom gives you *options,* such as — deciding what *you* want to do on a daily basis, without having to ask for someone else's approval. Options like — going on a trip when you want to, with as much money as you desire, for as long as you want to stay. Options like — taking your children to school so you can spend more time with them. Options like — buying something you want because you like it, not just because the price was right. Options. Options. Options.

This Sounds Good, But...

It's likely you've had to work hard to get where you are and for most everything you have. Even so, you may not be where you want to be or have all you want to have. So you might be thinking that this business sounds too good to be true. Perhaps you're even asking yourself if this is really a good opportunity for you to make the changes you'd like to make.   You may be new to both the business and e-commerce, so that's understandable.

It helps to know who you'd be associating with in this business.   What companies has it attracted to provide products and services? We're often judged by the company we keep. Remember your parents being concerned about who you were hanging around with? Perhaps you have those same concerns with your children. Well, look who's "hanging around" this business. Many top corporations are either supplying, or affiliating with this powerful distribution opportunity.   They see the possibilities of aligning with a business that brings them closer to the consumer without the massive expense of advertising.

Great companies like MCI, Sony, Wrangler, Reebok, Panasonic, Kleenex, Rubbermaid, Kelloggs, Sunbeam, RCA, and scores of other Fortune 500's, as well as hundreds of other well-established companies, have seen the value of bringing their products to consumers this way. You can be certain all these companies did a great deal of research and forecasting before they ever ventured ahead with this concept. These companies are obligated to their stockholders to maximize profits and would consider only a well-calculated risk with a high potential for gain.

Overcoming The Fear Of Something New

Some of your friends, relatives, and associates, may not understand why you want to build your own business. Some may even be jealous of your wanting to move ahead. You simply may not get the support you had hoped for. These reactions are perfectly normal and they're all based on fear. Some people let their fear prevent them from seeking a way to better provide for their family. Who loses? They do.

To overcome any negative effect from these retorts, ask yourself this, "Do any of those people pay my bills?" Anyone who steps out and does anything different, stirs up feelings in others. They may start questioning their own day-to-day "rut" and may not like what they discover. They may be bored to death with their daily "grind" and yet scared to step out like you are. Afterall, as the saying goes, "it takes guts to leave the ruts." Congratulations for wanting to move-on! It shows you believe there is more to life.

Sometimes others who are "dumping" on us, instead of supporting us, get left by the wayside. When you're committed to accomplishing your dreams you may need to stay away from naysayers. Or, at the very least, ask that they either support you or not mention the subject.

Try To Claw Your Way To The Top Or Be "Carried" — It's Your Choice

Most people would like to consider themselves as being successful. Yet only a few can honestly say they've "made it." One reason for that could be that they're trying to do it alone. Perhaps they get on the corporate ladder and begin trying to climb to the top. Along the way they may get passed over for a promotion, let go due to a merger or downsizing, replaced by someone who'll work for less, or simply grow tired of the grind. Then they try to justify their lack of success by telling themselves, "It's lonely at the top." But they somehow fail to notice how crowded it is at the bottom!

How Would You Answer These Three Questions?

For many people considering taking advantage of what this business has to offer, three questions often come to mind. The first is almost always, **"Will it work?"** By now, you've read about some of the companies involved, you've learned a few of the principles of succeeding at this, and it's likely you've met some fine people. If so, they can introduce you to others who've had success and you can learn a great deal from them.

Still have doubts? As was mentioned earlier, nothing works — people work! This business is just an opportunity for people to work toward their dreams. And the Internet is a tremendous tool, but it's only useful when you work with people and take advantage of its power.

The second question most people ask is, **"Can I do it?"** Let's answer that by taking a brief look at exactly what "it" is.

To help you understand the basic ideas behind this business, here's a list of questions for you to answer regarding what you can and can not do. When you're finished, you'll have a pretty good idea of your potential in this business.

Can you...

- ◆ Purchase products and services from yourself, that you're already buying from some other business?
- ◆ Buy at a wholesale or discounted price rather than pay retail like you did at the "regular" stores?
- ◆ Share the opportunity with those who want more out of life?
- ◆ Share the products and services with those who want to save time and money?
- ◆ Help others share the opportunity, products and savings with people you meet?
- ◆ Log onto the Internet or learn how?
- ◆ Telephone an e-mail service, hook your TV to a web service, or go to your public library — if you don't have a computer?
- ◆ Duplicate this process again and again?

"Can you do it?" When your dream is big enough, and you focus on it and do whatever it takes to make it happen, you could honestly answer "yes."

But, the third and most important question you need to answer is, **"*Why* would I do it?"** In other words, what's your dream? What do you really, really, really want? What would cause you to take action? The power of the Internet and the successful history of this opportunity is only information for conversation unless you take action. This business gives you a vehicle in which you can apply yourself to make your dreams come true. The people who become great successes in life, first and foremost, know *why* they want to do something. Simply put, they have a dream!

Are You Living Your Dream?

Only you can answer that. And be honest with yourself. If you're not living your dream, it's probably because you're either not in a vehicle that makes it possible, or not doing what it takes. But with the opportunity of this business, coupled with the awesome power of the Internet, you now know you can never say you haven't been given a chance.

You've just read about what many business leaders consider as one of the most exciting opportunities in the world for anyone to get ahead. But it's up to you to do something with it. Nobody's going to twist your arm...the choice is yours. This is simply a vehicle for you to get what you want out of life.

Technology is continuing to change and offer people the opportunity to improve their lives. You can take advantage of these breakthroughs and grow a business that can provide opportunities for nearly anyone who chooses to participate. You may be the only one who ever offers someone the chance to have a more successful life. And when you give that chance to enough "someones," and help them succeed, your success is virtually assured.

Today there are many people living their dream, and so can you. *If not this, what? If not now, when?* Remember,

"...Only you have the final say in what you become and how you live your life."

Epilogue

Are you excited? As you read the last few pages of this book, be excited by the possibilities that exist for you. Seize this opportunity and create levels of success that you have not reached before. Go out and make a difference in the lives of people who never really believed they had a chance at success. To me, that's the ultimate excitement. I hope all of you have the opportunity to meet someone whose life gets better because of what you do.

And just think...this is only the beginning! Even though people have been building their own businesses for years, a new benchmark has been set. Now with the Internet — and the established system in place — you have the opportunity to soar to heights that have never been reached before.

You can have a new future. You can begin a new journey and build a life you may have never believed possible before. Focus on those things and you'll be on your way to success. Any challenges along the way will feel like tiny bumps in the road, and soon be forgotten.

Continue to recharge yourself. Keep investing in yourself by reading positive books, listening to positive tapes, and attending any functions sponsored by the leadership in your business. As long as you continue doing this, you'll attract others who will want to invest in you as well.

Share what you attain. As you prosper, give to the organizations and causes you believe in, and remember to share your knowledge as well. Not just about the business as an opportunity but also share the positive changes you have experienced. If someone chooses not to participate, don't shut him or her out as a friend. Care about them by giving them the opportunity to change their mind later on.

Those who understand what needs to be done just need to go out and do it. Those who believe they have their hands on something special but can't quite get themselves going, may want to reread this book, and get together with their leader or mentor, or the person who shared this book with them.

I hope you can now better see the possibilities that lie ahead for you, and embrace the challenges that come your way.

Ultimately, the most important thing you can do with this business is share it with other people. Take action and better your life. The person who shared this book with you thought enough about you and your potential, and believed you could benefit from this opportunity. But, only you can decide what to do with it. It's totally up to you. And...

You Can Do It!

About The Author

John Fuhrman is first and foremost a husband and father. He is also a speaker, peak performance trainer, business consultant, and bestselling author. He is the founder and president of *Frame of Mind, Inc.,* an organization dedicated to the motivation, activation, and performance enhancement of his clients. He has been an award winning sales producer, manager, and entrepreneur. He is also a member of the National Speakers Association, and a noted authority on rejection.

John is dedicated to helping people achieve their dreams. He has helped improve the performance of thousands of independent business owners and professionals through his books and speaking programs. His books are written with a special sensitivity to help people grow their businesses and further their personal development.

He is a sought after speaker and author on success and motivation, as well as on sales and leadership. He lives with his wife, Helen, and their two children, John and Katie.